The Forward Book of Poetry

2022

The Forward Book of Poetry

2022

First published in Great Britain by
Forward Arts Foundation,
in association with
Faber & Faber · Bloomsbury House · 74-77 Great Russell Street
London WC1B 3DA

ISBN 978 0 571 36940 9 (paperback)

Compilation copyright © Forward Arts Foundation 2021
Foreword copyright © James Naughtie
Preface copyright © William Sieghart
Cover copyright © Patrick Fisher

Typeset by Avon DataSet Ltd, Alcester, Warwickshire B49 6HN

Printed and bound by CPI Group (UK) · Croydon CR0 4YY

A CIP catalogue reference for this book
is available at the British Library

To Robyn Marsack

Contents

The Forward Prize for Best Single Poem
   Shortlisted poems

Highly Commended Poems 2021

Foreword

Poetry in a time of contagion. The 30th year of the Forward Prizes finds us looking at ourselves differently, as if we've been thrown together – and kept apart – in a way that we couldn't have imagined before we began to hear talk of the virus and felt the first prickle of alarm. Therefore, poets, who explore our fragility and try to identify the hidden strengths that last, weave an important strand in our thinking about what has happened – not in the sorting out of fact and fiction in the public debate, nor in the argument about who in government was right or wrong at a particular moment, but in shining light on who we are. The question has been put to all of us in a startling new way.

Loneliness. Distance. Communal fear. A search for handholds in the past. They are themes poets have teased out in good times as well as bad. One of the fascinations for this year's judges was in looking at work that had been conceived before the pandemic began – perhaps long before – and discovering how penetrating it could be about life in lockdown, or about grief and loss, in a way that took on as much meaning as those lines that were produced after the world started to change in 2020. That was an exhilarating task because it was a reaffirmation of what the poetic imagination can do in explaining the here and now from somewhere else.

It's commonplace now to talk about the era represented by the Forward Prizes as a 'good time for poetry' (not least because of the prizes' own role in finding and nurturing talent), but each year it's important that the case is made again. There are still too many people who wouldn't think of picking up a book of contemporary poetry, or of looking for that half-hidden shelf in the charity bookshop and who know little of what they're missing. Performance poets have certainly found themselves with a wider stage than before, and there's a generation that finds it easy to think of poetry as an extension of music without erecting artificial barriers. But evangelism (of the best kind) is still needed.

Anyone exploring the lines in this collection will find refreshment. Some of it will be reassuring, and some of it disturbing. Your emotions might be stirred by the contours of an ancient landscape, by trees that take on a meaning for the lives that encircle them, by the sheer force of a transformation in the natural world. Or by the noise and smell of the urban cacophony, in which solitude is as likely as it is on an upland moor.

Or by the deceptions, innocent or malign, that often shape our days.

You'll be taken on journeys to distant worlds and familiar places, feel the pulse of the passing days on the land or the crackle of street life on the North Peckham estate in south London. Rediscover Shakespeare's sonnets – as if for the first time – through prose poems that take a leap from those great lines. Wander into hospitals and schools and kitchens and into dark corners where the lonely and the fearful find themselves hiding away. Hear voices for the first time. Discover feelings that you thought you had lost.

These poems represent the collections that have risen to the top of the pile this year, but they also reveal how the necessary judgements in awarding prizes – and let's be clear that there is nothing wrong in celebrating the best – mustn't be allowed to conceal the richness that spreads through the work that was submitted by dozens of poets and mustn't be lost. There are gems scattered everywhere: an image, a line, a cadence, even just a word in the perfect place that lodges in the memory. The eventual winners are in these pages but so is other work that deserves a wider readership.

The judges had to balance that pleasure with the difficult choices that produced the shortlists for the Best Collection, the Best First Collection and the Best Individual Poem. This year, my fellow judges were three poets and a critic steeped in contemporary poetry. Leontia Flynn teaches at Queen's University Belfast, where she is Reader at the Seamus Heaney Centre; she has published four collections of her own work. Pascale Petit, who trained as a sculptor, is the author of eight volumes of poetry, the last of which was shortlisted for Best Collection in the Forward Prizes 2020. They were joined from Trinidad by Shivanee Ramlochan, essayist and critic as well as poet, who is a moving force in the rich literary scene of the Caribbean. The panel was completed by Tristram Fane Saunders, poetry critic of the *Daily Telegraph*, whose work has appeared in many literary publications. Their commitment to the adventure of poetry produced a debate that was not only impassioned, because they found themselves moved by so much of the work, but also cool and decisive. Identifying true originality and an authentic literary voice needs serious thought as well as an open emotional response.

But I am not going to rank the poems in these pages. That's for the reader, for anyone who picks up this volume and sets off on the journey.

Their styles vary enormously, from the short and diamond-sharp to the dreamy and the emotionally raw. From the lyrical to the raucous. But all of them produce their own explosion of thought and feeling, and each will leave its own distinctive traces long after you've turned the page.

It will take time for us to understand how we've been changed by the events of the pandemic. Curiously, we've been compelled to think more deeply about what community means while at the same time having to experience solitude, or at least the constraints of a locked-down life, in a way that many of us had previously been able to avoid. It's hard to think of more fertile soil for poetry. Whether or not it was written with knowledge about what was coming, or what it brought into our homes, these are the eternal questions that poets can never put aside. How do we survive as individuals? How do we deal with each other? What do we learn from the world around us, from the permanent landscape we inherit and the one we build for ourselves?

If it's true that the counterbalance to the economic privations brought on by the pandemic will be a certain kind of spiritual refreshment – perhaps a feeling that we somehow have to start all over again – then poetry will be part of it. If we don't use our imagination and respond to its rhythms, how can we expect to be better for the experience? That's why poets like the ones represented in these pages are important to us all. Their grasp of the magic of words and the alchemy that results is not only sustenance but inspiration.

For three decades, the Forward Prizes have championed our greatest poets and helped to bring more readers and listeners to the new voices that are their successors. This anthology is another step on that never-ending journey. It is sad and hilarious, shocking and reassuring, puzzling and inspiring. Everything we are and hope to be.

James Naughtie
Chair of the judges
May 2021

Preface

Shahidha Bari, the 2019 Forward Prizes chair of judges, wrote: 'Deep in our reading, it became clear how often our writers reached to poetic forms to capture individual experiences of trauma and collective experiences of tragedy.' The *Guardian* likewise observed in January 2021, 'to express the grief and dislocation of our times, only poems will do'.

This year's esteemed chair of judges, James Naughtie, has said artfully how this volume speaks for our times. But I pick up his call to evangelise: if ever we were in need of poetry, surely it's now. After 20 surreal months of the coronavirus pandemic, coupled with the righteous rising of the Black Lives Matter protests, our collective need for understanding only grows.

Poetry is about connection: a poet takes up a pen and gives a glimpse of their world, and we see a sliver reflected in our own. We take that poem and share it with someone, and they find something perhaps entirely different but equally relevant, and on, and on. That current of thought – conversations across miles and continents – is able to bridge the walls that divide us and to bind us together wherever we are.

Perhaps that's why poetry surged in popularity during the coronavirus pandemic. At Forward, we have seen direct evidence of its ascendance. By June 2020, National Poetry Day had more traffic to the website than all of 2019, and we reached 131 million people on the day itself. Since March 2020, we've supported the poet Liv Torc in her #haiflu project, which got some 2.3 million people writing and sharing haikus alongside images of lives locked down. The digital prizes ceremony in October 2020 secured our biggest audience yet, and we offered a trove of in-depth conversations with last year's shortlist through our digital Meet the Poets series.

Poetry swooped into our lives because it is agile, inclusive and responsive to the thunderous changes of the last year. It could quell the panic, or at least let us feel less alone with it.

Holly Hopkins – who guided these prizes through the shortlisting phase before maternity leave – said the hardest thing about judging in Zoom-times is that you miss out on the tea breaks, when judges console each other that a beloved book did not make the shortlist. For every book and poem celebrated here, there are many more that will be spoken of over tea kettles and, hopefully, soon in live venues as well as digital gathering places.

This year we had more entries than ever before – 231 books compared with 208 in 2020, and the Best Single Poem entries held steady at 202. I thank the judges – James Naughtie, Leontia Flynn, Pascale Petit, Shivanee Ramlochan and Tristram Fane Saunders – for their commitment and care in reading this selection, and for their thoughtful, brave and lively debate, even at pain of Zoom fatigue.

Thank you, too, to Lucy Coles and everyone at our sponsors, Bookmark – the content marketing agency. Bookmark have supported us from the very start: their commitment over the past 30 years is an example to all in literary sponsorship.

Huge thanks to Melanie Curtis and Andy Ramsbottom at Avon Dataset who typeset this book, and to Jude Gates at Faber & Faber, who helped coordinate print production. Thanks to Sophie Blacksell Jones, John Clegg and Rachel Piercey, who have been intimately involved in the making of the book. The cover is the work of Patrick Fisher.

We are grateful to Arts Council England, the Esmée Fairbairn Foundation, and to the estate of the late Felix Dennis – which supports the Felix Dennis Prize for Best First Collection. Thank you, too, to my fellow trustees of the Forward Arts Foundation: Martin Thomas, Giles Spackman, Kim Evans and Jamie Andrews.

Thanks to the Foundation's staff, particularly Holly Hopkins, the Forward Prizes manager; Harriet MacMillan, who's bravely stepped into the role on secondment from Creative Scotland; Mónica Parle, the executive director, and Natalie Charles, operations manager.

Most especially the Forward team wants to thank Susannah Herbert, the previous executive director, who steered this enterprise for eight game-changing years. This collection – and so much of what we'll go on to achieve – speaks to your legacy.

William Sieghart
Founder of the Forward Prizes for Poetry
June 2021

The Forward Book of Poetry

2022

Shortlisted Poems
The Forward Prize for Best Collection

Kayo Chingonyi

The last night of my 20s

for Roddy Lumsden

Fitting that the day should dawn
in this most Lumsdenesque of Lumsdenesque
contexts: sea-froth for night music
and the company of Suzannah –
kind enough to show me this walk
she knows without recourse to light.

When the hour came
'Mr Brightside' played it in
a song to which
      by dint of the glint
            in Sophie Barnard's eye
               twelve years ago
I cannot listen passively.

Which calls to mind the secret canticle
that undoes you, Roderick.
Maybe it is better some things
retain their mist
that all of us might carry a well of myth
in the pit of our pith,
maybe it is by such melodies we exist.

Origin Myth – Miguel

After dancing in clubs that never close
his allegiance is to a Hammond B3
that, if you play it right, will disclose,
by sympathetic magic of its stuck key,
the traces of a blacker melody.

After church he plays the devil's music,
fingers tap a boogie-speckled blues riff
in praise of fingertips brushing a nose,
deliberate, a darkened corner's hungry
trysts, hips scoring the music's crescendos.

Accustomed to underlay, the seedy
sides of town, he favours bars whose heady
mix of high and low he finds therapeutic
(acquaintance with the night has its uses).

Tishani Doshi

After a Shooting in a Maternity Clinic in Kabul

No one forgets there's a war going on,
but there are moments you could be forgiven
for believing the city is still an orchard,
a place where you could make a thing grow.
There is always a pile of rubble from which
some desperate person struggles to rise,
while another person wraps a shawl
around their shoulders and roasts
marshmallows over a fire.
This is not that.
This is not bomb dropping from sky,
human shield, hostages in a stream, child
picking up toy that explodes in her hands—
although there's always that—hope is a booby trap.
This is the house you were brought to after crossing
a river, leaving the mountains and burnt fields
behind. A place of safety where you
could be alone with your own
startling power.
Not *Why were you out? And why
wasn't your face covered? And who told you
to climb into that rickshaw?* But here, prepare
for this most ordinary thing, a birth. And this is not
to ask what it means to never see someone again,
but to ask what it means not to make it past
the first checkpoint of your mother's gates.
Never mind all the wild places
outside—
the mud-brick villages, the valleys and harvests
and glasses of green tea. Or even to say, *I am here
to claim the child of Suraya* because you know
this to be impossible. Even if you could bring a man
to recover your sister's corpse and the newborn,

where do you go from here? You still have
to consider the bodies, the bullet-ridden
walls, still have to find the small
window of this house and take
in the panorama.
See—it is raining outside and men weep
for their wives, and perhaps the entire world
is an orchard that has detonated its crimson fruits,
its pomegranates and poppies and tart mulberries
to wash these floors red, and those of us who stand
outside this house know that nothing will flourish
here again. Like crowds who gather
for an execution, we can only ask,
what does it mean to be born
in a graveyard, to enter
the world, saying,
oh thief, oh life.

Mandala

Anyone who believes a leaf is just a leaf is missing
the point. In the attic, there's a picture of ginkgo
growing steadily yellow, while the body
of ginkgo remains evergreen. He works his way
through opium dens and bordellos. I'd like to tell you
not to worry. Reality has a way of sorting itself out,
but panic is infectious. The scare arrives when you're doing
jumping jacks or organising the cutlery, some moment of low
cosmological drama. Interrupted by the discovery of a lump.
Or the 9 o'clock news. Suddenly, every door handle is a death
sentence. How lonely it must have been for the first astronomers,
freezing on their terraces, trying to catch the light of faraway moons.
Sometimes it's hard to know whether you're slowing down
or speeding up. Time's wobbly trampoline confuses us.
We stitch our days and nights, one to the other,
and it's like embroidering a galaxy, but even galaxies
recede from one another. Once, a woman played my body
as though it were a harp. I slept on a wooden plank
and she strummed the strings below until I became
a whale shark, pounding through the oceans. I emerged
as if out of a wormhole, more or less intact. For days I felt fins
where my cheeks should have been. We talk of bodies
as though we could not understand the universe within them,
even though we've all gaped at the stump of a tree
and understood that time moves outwards in a circle.
And while everything seems endless, there's always a ring
of something permeable holding us in. Sometimes we leave
the house without our masks and it's a relief to take a break
from who we are. Dwarf star, prayer bell, lone stag
feeding in the gorse—something will hold a mirror
to our faces, when all we need is to be led upstairs.

Selima Hill

The Beautiful Man Whose Name I Can't Pronounce

I can but it's so beautiful I don't.
I prefer to think it's unpronounceable,

to go to bed and think of him as fruit
glimpsed at night by someone who is lost,

who walks for many days, weighed down by maps
and dictionaries and old pronunciation guides

until she's so exhausted and confused
she can't pronounce the name of where she's going to,

never mind the name of the fruit
into whose fat cheeks she dreams she's biting.

Wedding Cake

So tall, so bored, so irresistible,
he's not so much a man as a wedding cake –

a wedding cake that deep inside its icing
is concentrating on not thinking *knife*.

Luke Kennard

'How heavy do I journey on the way' (50)

She had two horses: an Appaloosa to ride towards nice things or away from bad things; and an American Quarter Horse to ride towards anything she didn't want to do, or to ride away from nice things when it was time to do so. I would dutifully ride whichever horse she wasn't using at the time, sneaking it Polo mints, because the system required that both horses always be present, whatever the affair. I was not a good horse-rider but had accepted my obligations as what you get for marrying "up". My boots were a size too small. I loved the smell of mud in the cool night air. The happy horse was so happy and the sad horse was so sad. One night the sad horse saw an angel blocking our path and was temporarily granted the gift of speech. She was riding ahead on the happy horse and didn't notice. The sad horse told me a story about scientists working to slow down an asteroid on a collision course with Earth. It imagined it was one of the scientists delivering the news after the plan had failed. 'It's still accelerating,' the sad horse had to say to the government, 'but it's not accelerating as fast as it was; forgive us for seeing that as a victory.' 'So it's getting *faster?*' the Chancellor of the Exchequer would say. 'Yes,' the horse would reply. 'It's just not getting faster as quickly as it was before.'

'Then let not winter's ragged hand deface' (6)

I had a dream that there were ten of you and we lived in a duplex overlooking the river. It was the only nice part of town. I wanted to make ten of you happy, but it was difficult and mostly I felt like I was letting at least eight of you down. Even though the ten of you were exactly you and exactly the same, you cannot stroke ten people's hair and tell them they are good, they are so good, and oh the divergent seconds where lived experience changed you. Even the inanities, *I love what you've done to your hair. Is that a new top? Could you just shift over a little?* I didn't think I was up to the job. So this is a *job* for you? I don't want to make any special claims here: nobody ever walked down to a river without at least considering taking a dive. We only owned nine mugs, for instance, and it only struck me years later, snow-fishing in a void I'd learned to wrap around myself, how easy it would have been for me to do something about that.

Stephen Sexton

The Curfew

The radicals sprung the locks that night, hurrah!
and their lovely collarbones were almost moonly.

Rhinos shrieked and bellowed, elephants tromboned
and the animals nosed into town.

Sunrise to sunrise and sunrise we kept indoors.
If you can't count your onions, what can you count

my grandfather used to say. He said a lot of things.
Among the other miners he was legendary:

when no more than the thought of the pink crumple
of his infant daughter's body came to mind

a glow would swell in the pit, the men
would mayhem bauxite by the light

his tenderness emitted.
Some of me lived inside her even then.

The memorial fountain says nothing
of the weeks before the rescue failed

but mentions God which, as my grandfather
used to say, is just the name of the plateau

you view the consequences of your living from.
Or something like that. He said a lot of things.

He grew wise and weary as an albatross
and left for that great kingdom of nevertheless.

It would have pleased his handsome shoulders
to watch this grizzly scoop for salmon

in the fountain of his friends, or the Bengals,
or the shakedown squad of chimpanzees

who bang and bang on the grocery window.
One by one eleven miners starved to death.

In the streets they collar or tranquillise
the ocelots and run a spike of ketamine

through the plumbing in the fountain.
Dromedaries blue-mood around the pub

aloof under their reservoirs of fat.
I don't sleep, but oh plateau! these days

of violence have been my happiest.
Even a cabbage is not without desire

my grandfather said one day, and now
among the animals, I feel under my wings

the words for things I thought I knew
departing, and I understand him.

High School Musical

Milquetoast isn't the word – retiring,
diffident, wouldn't say boo to a goose.
However it happened, he was transformed:
six brass buttons on his double-breasted
prop naval officer's jacket glinted
in the stage lights and the boatswain's whistle
he brought to attention his children with
could be heard in this life and the next.

In those days I looked up to him, wooden,
kissing Maria not quite on the mouth.
In those days I was his right hand.
While he dumb-thumbed a Spanish guitar
and sang *Edelweiss* for the fatherland,
I hunched on a stool in the orchestra pit
and waltzed through the ache in my forearms.
Von Trapp fled Europe for America.

Mountains were unfastened and folded,
violinists slackened their bow hairs,
handshakes grew infrequent. After the show
I felt such an emptiness; I wanted
nebuchadnezzars of sweet Alsatian Riesling
to toast and swill with the Captain and crew,
but he was the sort for a prayer before bed
and a tick in the box marked *extracurricular*.

I expect he married and volunteered
for a mission in Zimbabwe or Chad,
and went on about water into wine
or the one about the wheat and the chaff,
until the miracles of nighttime and shame
brought twins each splendider than the other
and the big subpoena of the Lord
called him home to his native parish.

The last time I saw Daniel, a decade
thence, he was preaching brimstone
and worse from the bandstand
with a captain's steel and bearing.
I must be born again, Daniel, I know,
but wouldn't it be my luck
to be born into a golden age goldener
than the afterlife: so lovely, and so fucked.

Shortlisted Poems
The Felix Dennis Prize for Best First Collection

Caleb Femi

Boys in Hoodies

The inside of a hoodie is a veiled nook where a boy pours himself
into a single drop of rain to feed a forest. Each tree grateful for the
wet boy, unaware that the outside world sees this boy as a
      chainsaw.

Have you heard the canned laughter of a chainsaw? Don't listen
      for it
in forests, amid the ankles of trees, or the tongue of dried leaf.

Listen in the vibration of pavements when the concrete is wax,
outside of a Morley's where one chainsaw says to the other,
'member that time when

(gas)

    (gas)

and the money was in his socks?

Then a rip of laughter like the chugger of iron
              or heavy rain
              erupts –

and nearby trees brace for death or life.

Things I Have Stolen

From the highest shelf
my tiptoes could reach me
I stole a Mars bar & Haribo sweets.
It wasn't a big deal: Mum said
their prices were a robbery anyway.

Later years, Marusha stole my heart,
jerked it out through the ribcage.
In desperation I stole another,
then another. Then a few more:
Fatima, Rihanna, Andrea.
Better to have and not need, I thought,
than need and not have.

Aylesbury estate, I saw Kevin steal Frank's
white Air Force Ones. Do you know how long
it takes a fourteen-year-old yout to save
enough Ps to buy those trainers?
Kevin stole Frank's soul, plucked it
like fruit in a swaying tree.

And I thought, what a game changer:
if Kevin can steal a soul, what else can be stolen?
So I stole the flavour from water
and I stole the solar eclipse.

Then I stole my torn name from the mouth
of the policeman who stops
and searches me
every week. Stole hunger pangs
from underneath our bed, at night.
Six years went by. At Kevin's funeral
I reached into the air
and stole the family's grief.

Alice Hiller

o dog of pompeii

your howl was buried under
metres of ash and pumice

torched belly up then cast into stained
plaster from your void of terror

I want to say who bent your neck
how was your arse split

I want to release that studded collar
chained hound of my underworld

o dog of pompeii

you writhe beside forty lucky roman charms
laid out in their glass coffin

taken from the bracelet of the burnt child
found curled on vesuvius's shoreline

whose hunched body carries me back
to the linen sheets and lace counterpane

in my mother's house where the garden
hides dark sheds hung with limp pheasants

where rhododendrons flash
slippery purple pleasures

where the dead eye of the bird bath
looks up   but sees nothing

o dog of pompeii

you turned your head away
while my mother unhooked her corset

and did not dare to growl
or bare your teeth to guard

when I first entered the fish smell
where my mouth tasted wet flesh hair

where I lost you   beloved playmate
as a finger   moved inward

forcing me   whimpering
down warrens   of dark tunnels

o dog of pompeii

here amongst the erotic statues
and carbonised cradles

I find you at last   brought back to me whole
mosaiced to life   and risen again

asking me to throw this red rubber ball
and watch you rush towards it barking

mosaics of guard-dogs have
been found in many houses
in pompeii and herculaneum
reminding guests this was a
protected space

valentine

a china heart
enamelled with violets

lies in a leather box
lined with silk

the heart shuts
with a golden clasp

on a doily
these words

I once belonged
to someone dear

note: this memory comes shagged with flies

I went down into the pit
conjectured to have been an
amphitheatre all were adorned
with grotesques

Cynthia Miller

Sonnet with lighthouses

The first lighthouse is you.

The second lighthouse is you, age 12, turned around beneath a wave.

The third lighthouse is a hyperbaric chamber you clamber into when you dive too deep and rise too fast, an oil-dark depth that's child's play for trained divers but you, girl, you clawed yourself up –

The fourth lighthouse tunes into the shipping song over sea static: rain later, good, occasionally poor.

The fifth lighthouse says over and over, I love you I love you I love you you you you there.

Every wall in the sixth lighthouse is load-bearing.

The seventh lighthouse is a scattergram of light that indicates the strength and direction between two variables: ship and safe harbour, moon and tide, shore and vagaries of current, each of us to each other, our future selves to our past selves, every dear friend placed at strategic vantage points in our life.

Just seeing the eighth lighthouse strengthens your circuitry, blood zinging around your bones in delight.

The ninth lighthouse has *worse things happen at sea* cheerfully cross-stitched on a pillow it bought drunk off Etsy.

The tenth lighthouse sometimes just wants to be a lifeboat or a ladder or an oxygen mask, dropped down in case of emergencies and not always looking out for other people when they can't help themselves.

The eleventh lighthouse's favourite piece of furniture is the walnut drop-leaf table that opens so everyone can fit around it.

The twelfth lighthouse makes you feel like stepping out of time.

The thirteenth lighthouse comforts you with Fermat's mathematical proof which shows that light knows where it's going, that it takes the shortest possible route, even through water and gale forces.

The fourteenth lighthouse hollers MARCO.
                                        POLO, everyone you love shouts back.

To become a dragon first wear its skin

When she married, my mother wore a cheongsam
of red silk bright as a bolt of dragonfire. Her mother
tipped her from the bath and poured her into it, all
brimstone brilliance and the hottest part of the flame.
The tailoring perfect, each button knotted and curled
like a dragon's whiskers, and she liked that it was a touch
demure but slitted high enough on the thigh to turn heads.
The cool material felt like slipping out at night
to lie on your back in the sea, or the drawn-out pleasure
of a cigarette after sex, sheets pooled in the sticky heat.
Shoes, of course, buckled dragonskin. Imagine a bride,
knowing she could swallow any man whole. And later,
imagine a newlywed, packing a bag for his things
(coarse denim jacket stinking of hay and Oreo nicotine smell),
and finding the cheongsam at the back of the wardrobe,
pressed and forgotten. She cards her fingers through
whispering tissue, remembers the dress clinging like smoke.
Imagine memory as a whetstone. She sharpens herself on it.

Holly Pester

Blood

My mother told everyone in the village
and at the local art college that she'd die for a blood
velvet cake in the shape of a house. All day I received
and hid progressively larger eventually
life-sized blood cake houses. The art students made the
biggest and most ambitious. It didn't fit in my camera
scope. She can always fake cry. Especially in my camera scope.
The local paper asked how amazed she was.
This is worse than the time she got several abused ponies.
She turned to me and whispered how extremely creepy and
artistic it was for the villagers to do this. The next morning
she lay down on a raft while her anxious friend oared her out to sea.

Villette

In the novel *Villette*, either I or Lucy Snowe live and work in a girls' school that either she or I found in a small French town. She has nowhere / I have nowhere and no thing in which to hide any of her few / my few possessions. Her mattresses / my mattresses and bedding in the dormitory where she sleeps / I sleep are checked over daily, and she suspects / I suspect that her / my desk in the classroom is also looked through.

She has nowhere / I have nowhere to hide a letter that was sent to her / to me by Dr Graham, who she has a heavy and imaginative crush on / who I have a heavy and imaginative crush on.

She invests / I invest in the letter a devotional adoration that mismatches the friendly goodwill it was written with.

I / Lucy guess that the schoolmistress has snatched, read and then returned the letter to under her / my bed. Lucy panics over her / my lack of private space and makes the eccentric decision to bury the letter in the garden grounds of the school.

She folds the pages tightly / I fold the pages tightly, wrap them in a silk handkerchief dipped in oil, curl them into a glass bottle and hermetically seal the bottle with wax.

She buries the bottle / I bury the bottle under the roots of an ivy bush in an area of the garden that is haunted by either me or the ghost of a nun who was buried alive.

In this gesture / in my gesture, Lucy Snowe rejects the possibility of possessing the letter. She applies / I apply a fantastical value to the letter. The letter passes into an earthed state of absence. I use / Lucy uses burial as a way to disown the letter and to refuse being privately subjected by the letter. She instead / I instead ecstatically ritualise her poverty / my poverty, and her otherness / my otherness to ownership of objects, and evacuate the self into love.

Ralf Webb

Aktiengesellschaft, Wiltshire

Green stuff has wormed its way up
through the mutilated tarmac
outside the main factory floor,
ultra-real in the neon warning lights.
New management have fortified protocol,
under the banner of 'efficiency'.
Lordly, alien, compulsory rules,
introduced by our friends
from Munich. Who visit occasionally.
Some of us walk to work. For others
home is an address spelled out
to a bank clerk. SEPA. BACS.
Easy enough to assemble. But when,
in free time, you feel impelled
to pick things apart, abstracts enter.
Like, Pete's looking at me funny, looks
kind of sinister, holding that spanner.
Is an accident ever an accident, or
a forced, subterranean lapse in judgement?
Automated warnings over the tannoy:
Do not attempt to clean the machine
from the inside. Do not attempt
to enter the machine. It's like they think
we're stupid. Who'd ever try that again?

Love Story: Crown of Love

There is too much grass to mow.
It's better to lie down in from time to time,
And get lost, clutching, for e.g.,
Your ankle, finally fitting a finger
Into the rim of your ear,
Finding dried blood there
From a miscellaneous fly sting
You might have picked at, and at. Show me
Where, exactly, inside of you
I can hide. I am desperate to hide,
Co-ordinates please, Jesus:
This is the most I have ever wanted.
Or, to peaceably scythe every false growth,
and grow again, from the inside out.

The tree-brains are shedding their pollen.
I am shedding all pretences, refining
My attentions. In a moment
Of lucidity, watching a black ant
Move up your knee, I am convinced
We could bury the artefacts
Of our respective sicknesses, back there
In the vegetable patch, to be nourished
By common minerals, and evolve.
Is this bad taste, selfish, the sense that
There are no more problems left to solve?
Nix to the global crises, the endless
Ecological traumas. Just, don't care.
Let the engines float, then tumble through the air.

What I'm saying is, the chips are down:
I tasted the copper of your body
And instantly handed over all
Of my amulets, for you to evaluate
One by one, and tell me how

To lower my guard. God, I can't deal:
These sort of sickeningly lovely
Scarlet foxgloves in late June
Arrowing themselves at the house,
Stephin Merritt playing on your phone.
The real, actual, terrifying fact
That we've cleared the mesh
Of countless afternoons, and just like that,
Have fallen into it, on your parents' lawn.

Shortlisted Poems
The Forward Prize for Best Single Poem

Fiona Benson

Androgeus

I died in Athens, thinking of my mother.
Or was I on my way to Thebes?
Difficult to say, this is a slow, forgetting place.
There was a competition, I had won –
something – a crown, a coin, a paper wreath?
Then stabbing pain – a bull's two horns,
or a bar-tab brawl, or an Athenian lover
I hadn't treated well – daggering my lower abdomen.
Can it have been my father's white bull?
The one he bathed and preened? It doesn't matter now.
After the wound, came dying: fast then slow, slow, slow.
I had doctors and staunchings and stitches and fevers,
time to dream about the sun-scorched cliffs of Crete,
the sweetness of the singing crickets,
the way the thyme would twist and bake,
how my lover's skin smelt of it, how
when I took him in my mouth he'd grip my hair
and groan and move me to his pleasure
and forget I was the prince. Afterwards
I'd lie with my cheek on his warm chest
and watch the fish shoal in the water far below,
every stone and crab's claw, every sea urchin's thorn
delineated… There came a peace like that, at last,
when everything seemed clear and calm and bright,
and I was sitting on the warm stone step
with my mother, eating a dish of cold yoghurt
laced with honey, and she was singing
a soft and faraway song in her other tongue;
she laughed and mussed my hair
and blew on my nape to cool my neck.
And then I died.

Natalie Linh Bolderston

Middle Name with Diacritics

Linh hồn [soul]

1. A voice / tapping / from inside the skin
2. Quan Âm / the goddess of compassion / at the end of her ninth life / having shed the last stinging layer / of flesh
3. A temple full / of starving yellow birds
4. Ancestors / who stitch your prayers into houses / with the floors missing
5. The name of four teenage girls / in my mother's refugee camp
6. The part of me / often left out or misspelled / that moves quietly through the world

Lính [soldier]

1. Two sisters / who delivered a village from the throat / of a tiger / the Red River's champions / anointed as queens
2. A woman / their descendant / two hundred years later / who carried girls from the betrayal of moonlight / searched a field / for the skinless face / of someone she loved
3. Frenchmen / who guarded Bà Ngoại's school gates / when she was a girl / she cycled right up / in white áo dài / offered paper flowers / she had never heard / a foreign accent before
4. The ringing / in the ears / after a grenade / shreds open the morning
5. The rising tone of flesh / heavy with napalm
6. A man / who searches a crater / he made earlier / who returns to Huế many years later / touches reconstructions / of all he destroyed

Bản lĩnh [bravery]

1. A monk / whose heart will not burn / no matter the heat / whose words / tugged his spirit from his body / to watch over / the spectacle of suffering / the way a flower / opens to drought
2. A woman / hiding bribes in the walls / stops the shake of her hands / when she lies
3. A girl / in her parents' deserted house in Bạc Liêu / selling hats / waiting for word from her mother / hiding / from an older man / who has been watching her grow
4. A mother / bargaining / for broken rice / cubes of pork / cigarettes / ginger to help stomach her twelfth child / still inside her
5. A man / who lies on a table / on a boat / no anaesthetic / black powder medicine / the smell of burning
6. A girl again / in a camp / her fingers / on her sister's wrist through the night

Ra lịnh [to command]

1. A girl / who stops eating / asks her body to follow her / into silence
2. Bullets / at a teenage boy's heels / as he runs / from his uncle's seized field
3. Scripture / by unholy men / ordering Ông Ngoại to tame a jungle / into a home
4. Heirlooms surrendered / for silence / birthdates / sea / exile
5. Names given up / because home did not rest easily / on unyielding tongues
6. My mother's medicated bloodstream / that tells her / her pain does not exist / that her bones / have not yet lived through / all they can endure

John McCullough

Flower of Sulphur

X.   I love poetry but I love my friends more.

C.   *In frendship the absent be present, the nedie never lacke, the sicke thyncke them selves whole, and that which is hardest to be spoken, the dead never dye* (Cicero, *De Amicitia*, trans. John Harington, 1550).

S.   Friends *were* my twenties. Stuck for a Ph.D topic, I stayed inside a known city.

R.   *Much that seems effusive to the new scholar is routine.* Special *and* divine *friends abound* (John McCullough, *Disputable Friends: Rhetoric and Amicitia in English Renaissance Writing, 1579–1625*, 2005).

T.   You were the first friend to take a poetry course of mine. I thought, *This will be a test for me.*

W.   *Take an object from the bag and write about its weight and texture.*

P.   The humanist education system encouraged the keeping of commonplace books with strewn phrases, proverbs on friendship.

A.   *There are twenty-six objects, each linked to a letter of the alphabet. Who has A?*

F.   Lately, I've been stroking the limits of what I know, what I've forgotten; where this bleeds into what I've never understood.

B.   Francis Bacon compares friendship to the most painful remedies: Sarza *to open the* Liver; Steele *to open the* Spleene;

Flower *of* Sulphur *for the Lungs* (Bacon, 'Of Friendship', *Essayes*, 1625).

M. The Bag of Mysterious Objects is sorry. The course I taught you did not save your life.

Y. *Al thynges,* Laelius notes, *be by freendship kept togither, and by debate skattered: and this all menne bothe perceive, and prove in very deed* (Cicero, trans. Harington).

N. They found you in the bath, wrists opened. No note.

L. *There is no life without freendeshippe* (Ibid.).

J. You'd started learning Japanese. You were heading for Wakayama Prefecture in six months' time. No one knows what you planned to do there.

E. Laelius calls the prolonged mourning of a friend an error. *For a man to be grevously troubled for his owne losses, it is selfly love, and not frendly love* (Ibid.).

Q. I didn't go to your funeral. Why, I don't know. Whether this was wrong or right, I don't know.

H. Unable to write one Ph.D chapter, I had a breakdown, moved back in with my parents.

U. For five days after you died, it snowed and snowed. I built a white cat in my front garden, sticks for arms.

G. *He that beholdeth his friend, doeth as it wer behold a certain patterne of him selfe* (Ibid.).

D. The snowcat's arms dropped away in the night.

Z. In Wakayama, there is a shrine that has a yearly service for broken sewing needles that worked hard and now rest in a soft bed of tofu.

K. The signs of friendship do not mean as fully or securely as is expected of an ideal to be preferred *beefore all kynde of worldely thynges* (Ibid.).

V. After my viva, I lost all interest in Renaissance friends. I use my Ph.D as a doorstop.

I. Still, I stroke the gaps.

O. *The order of the alphabet is arbitrary*, you said. *Why not start at X?*

Denise Riley

1948

i

Your past can't tell it *is* the past.
How to convince it that it's done with, now?
The only touches that I got before I reached eighteen were blows.
It never crossed my mind to look for others' kindness, later on.
But my pigheaded will alone propelled me to my sorrows.

ii

When I could step into the shockingly open world
I wasn't sure of where I ended, or where someone else began.
This was a joyous state.
Under my skin I might have been a man, a kindly one.
Longing leaped in flames, it raced and crackled.
Small winds tore through it, keening
and fanning its chase.
It made the truest of songs –
it was the truth ablaze,
it was pure wanting, bloodied and radiant.
Holy, holy, sang that pursuit
and holier the infants born of it.
Then unholy the contempt that circled me.

iii

Time did, but did not, pass
in muted work and stabs of gaiety
to build some way for us to live
clear of the glaring, yet repeated, risks
of coupledom warped by rancour.
A darling can turn wolfish.

iv

I wished, half-helpfully, to be unseen
or run a website for the hard-to-place
with me as its founder member.
Now I'll brandish my rosy face around
teasing my pratfalls of a baffled need
while hope deferred still hollows me out,
takes clownish leaps about my gouged-out shell.

v

As there's dark humour in a darker time
so there's resilience in an obvious rhyme.

Self-parody deflates a plaintive mime
to make it truer – just *as* pantomime.

vi

The mothers are long dead,
the several fathers too.
What took place is done, though
it murmurs on in you
who got through it alive, with
a bit more extracting to do.

vii

On blackened streets the taint was scoured from doorsteps.
The illegitimate sent off to the infertile,
their pasts expunged, their names altered.
Their records sealed.
No need to mention any of it again.

That was only for the best, it was all for the best.
Everyone meant it for the best.

viii

This present-past hangs on. It says:
'Days flocked with frighteners – they'll circle round you still
though they're long dead who daily clouted you across the mouth –
*disgusting animal, you're asking for it, useless object, you want a good
thrashing.*
You didn't, but you got it anyway, with other things far better not
to get (though, decades later, getting pregnant saved your life
since you did get lovable children). Slaps smelled of bleach
striping your face in wheals each the width of the finger
that made them – you prayed that they'd fade before school.
A knee to the small of your back shoved you down
if you paused on the stairs: *you're bad – bad, through and through.*
You spend your next sixty-eight years working out how far that's true.
So what are you asking for now? To not still hear
these utterances, in the only mother tongue you knew:
*obey without question, you want a real beating, spare the rod
spoil the child, shut your gob or I'll shut it for you
you're neither use nor ornament, you're not like other girls
you don't deserve to be loved, you belong in the loony bin
a child has to have its spirit broken, hold your tongue
you disobedient animal, no one would ever believe you*
– Well, no. Though you'd never expected them to.
Who would have heard you then, who would,
since no one could see how you'd tried to be good.
You can't try any harder than ever you could.'

ix

'That couldn't have happened, you seem so normal.'
– I am so normal. And it did.
Just as it did to thousands.

I tell my past it's passed, though it can't tell.
More training, to teach obedience: the toddler
who'd wet herself gripped by the scruff of her neck
and her nose rubbed in it, in freshly damp white cotton.
Their real beloved dog I envied, while I stayed an 'it'
burrowing through straw quills in the kennel
to study the grace of the dog, to poach the secret of being liked.
Yet gradually my life as an 'it' has grown muscular.
Almost, I am that dog.

xi

I won't blame those enslaved by their own rages,
fearful of a baby that would never feel like theirs
yet couldn't be returned to the agency.
I blame the powers that packed us off to them
as misconceived children to be conformed –
easy mishaps in small border towns,
stains on their working families.

xii

Cast to the winds, some might find safe landings,
but others blew onto steel shards.
'Bad blood' was how our bad fortunes described us.
It could all have worked out fine – bar the tick
of a chancy official biro, handing you straight
to the care of gloved anger, or respectable angry anxiety.
But that was the luck of it, that was how it fell out
for surplus postwar children.
The indifferently falling rains of them.

xiii

'More care would get taken in re-homing a dog.'
Though the dog might at least have its pedigree.

Hit and miss (literally) where you ended up.
And each person involved was unknowing.

xiv

This history's too commonplace to tell.
It is a story which so many own.
How do I get it right, alone?
The point of telling is to crack its spell.

xv

'The point of telling is to crack its spell'?
What if it underscores dead violence
as calligraphy – a sentence
maybe freeing, but only if 'done well'?
And when the casual judgements fly
around each teller: 'She's damaged, TMI'?
– Judgment runs everywhere in our material.

Nicole Sealey

Pages 22–29
an excerpt from The Ferguson Report: An Erasure

These accounts are drawn entirely from officers' own descriptions, recorded in offense reports. That FPD officers believe criticism and insolence are grounds for arrest, and that supervisors have condoned such unconstitutional policing, reflects intolerance for even lawful opposition to the exercise of police authority. These arrests also reflect that, in FPD, many officers have no tools for de-escalating emotionally charged scenes, even though the ability of a police officer to bring calm to a situation is a core policing skill.

FPD officers also routinely infringe on the public's First Amendment rights by preventing people from recording **their** activities. The First Amendment "prohibit[s] the government from limiting the stock of information from which members of the public may draw." *First Nat'l Bank v. Bellotti*, 435 U.S. 765, 783 (1978). Applying this principle, the federal court of appeals have held that the First Amendment "unambiguously" establishes a constitutional right to videotape police activities. *Glik v. Cunniffe*, 655 F.3d 78, 82 (1st Cir. 2011); see also *ACLU v. Alvarez*, 679 F.3d 583, 600 (7th Cir. 2012) (issuing a preliminary injunction **against the** use of a state **eavesdrop**ping statute to prevent the recording **of** public police activities); *Fordyce v. City of Seattle*, 55 F.3d 436, 439 (9th Cir. 1995) (recognizing a First Amendme**n**t r**ight** to film police carrying out their public duties); *Smith v. City of Cumming*, 212 F.3d 1332, 1333 (11th Cir. 2000) (recognizing a First Amendment right "to photograph or videotape police conduct"). Indeed, as the ability to record police activity has become more widespread, the role it can play in capturing questionable police activity, and ensuring that the activity is investigated and subject to broad public debate, has become **clear**. Protecting civilian recording of police activity is thus at the core of speech the First Amendment is intended to protect. *Cf. Branzburg v. Hayes*, 408 U.S. 665, 681 (1972) (First

Amendment protects "news gathering"); *Mills v. Alabama*, 384 U.S. 214, 218 (1966) (news gathering enhances "free discussion of governmental affairs"). "In a democracy, public officials have no general privilege to avoid publicity and embarrassment by preventing public scrutiny of their actions." *Walker v. City of Pine Bluff*, 414 F.3d 989, 992 (8th Cir. 2005).

In Ferguson, however, officers claim without any factual support that the use of camera phones endangers officer safety. Sometimes, officers offer no rationale at all. Our conversations with community members and review of FPD records found numerous violations of the right to record police activity. In May 2014, an officer pulled over an African-American woman who was driving with her two sons. During the traffic stop, the woman's 16-year-old son began recording with his cell phone. The officer ordered him to put down the phone and refrain from using it for the remainder of the stop. The officer claimed this was "for safety reasons." The situation escalated, apparently due to the officer's rudeness and the woman's response. According to the 16-year-old, he began recording again, leading the officer to wrestle the phone from him. Additional officers arrived and used force to arrest all three civilians under disputed circumstances that could have been clarified by a video recording.

In June 2014, an African-American couple who had taken their children to play at the park allowed their small children to urinate in the bushes next to their parked car. An officer stopped them, threatened to cite them for allowing the children to "expose themselves," and checked the father for warrants. When the mother asked if the officer had to detain the father in front of the children, the officer turned to the father and said, "you're going to jail because your wife keeps running her mouth." The mother then began recording the officer on her cell phone. The officer became irate, declaring, "you don't videotape me!" As the officer drove away with the father in custody for "parental neglect," the mother drove after them, continuing to record. The officer then pulled over and arrested her for traffic violations. When the father asked the officer to show mercy, he responded, "no more mercy, since she wanted to videotape," and declared "nobody videotapes me." The officer then took the phone, which the couple's daughter was holding. After posting bond, the couple found that the video had been deleted.

A month later, the same officer pulled over a truck hauling a trailer that did not have operating **tail lights**. The officer asked for identification from all three people inside, including a 54-year-old white man in the passenger seat who asked why. "You have to have a reason. This is a violation of my Fourth Amendment rights," he asserted. The officer, who characterized the man's reaction as "suspicious," responded, "the reason is, if you don't hand it to me, I'll arrest you." The man provided his identification. The officer then asked the man to move his cell phone from his lap to the dashboard, "for my safety." The man said, "okay, but I'm going to record this." Due to nervousness, he could not open the recording application and quickly placed the phone on the dash. The officer then announced that the man was under arrest for Failure to Comply. At the end of the traffic stop, the officer gave the driver a traffic citation, indicated at the other man, and said, "you're getting this ticket because of him." Upon bringing that man to the jail, someone asked the officer what offense the man had committed. The officer responded, "he's one of those guys who watches CNBC too much about his rights." The man did not say anything else, fearing what else the officer might be capable of doing. He later told us, "I never dreamed I could end up in jail for this. I'm scared of driving through Ferguson now."

The Ferguson Police Department's infringement of individuals' freedom of speech and right to record has been highlighted in recent months in the context of large-scale public protest. In November 2014, a federal judge entered a consent order prohibiting Ferguson officers from interfering with individuals' rights to lawfully and peacefully record public police activities. That same month, the City settled another suit alleging that it had abused its loitering ordinance, Mun. Code § 29-89, to arrest people who were protesting peacefully on public sidewalks.

Despite these lawsuits, it appears that FPD continues to interfere with individuals' rights to protest and record police activities. On February 9, 2015, several individuals were protesting outside the Ferguson police station on the six-month anniversary of Michael Brown's death. According to protesters, and consistent with several video recordings from that evening, the protesters stood peacefully in the police department's parking lot, on the sidewalks in front of it, and across the street. Video footage shows that two FPD vehicles abruptly accelerated from the police parking lot into the street. An officer announced, "everybody here's going to jail," causing the protesters to run. Video shows that as one man recorded the police arresting others, he was arrested for interfering with police action. Officers pushed him to the ground, began handcuffing him, and announced, "stop resisting or you're **gon** g to g **e** t tased." It appears from the video, however, that the man was **neither interfering nor resisting**. A protester in a wheelchair who was live-streaming the protest was also arrested. Another officer moved several people with cameras away from the scene of the arrests, warning them against interfering and urging them to back up or else be arrested for Failure to Obey. The sergeant shouted at those filming that they would be arrested for Manner of Walking if they did not back away out of the street, even though it appears from the video recordings that the protesters and those recording were on the sidewalk at most, if not all, times. Six people were arrested during this incident. It appears that officers' escalation of this incident was unnecessary and in response to derogatory comments written in chalk on the FPD parking lot asphalt and on a police vehicle.

FPD's suppression of speech reflects a police culture that relies on the exercise of police power—however unlawful—to stifle unwelcome criticism. Recording police activity and engaging in public protest are fundamentally democratic enterprises because they provide a check on those "who are granted substantial discretion that may be misused to deprive individuals of their liberties." *Glik*, 655 F.3d at 82. Even **profane** back-talk can be a form of dissent against perceived misconduct. In the words of the Supreme Court, "[t]he **fre**edom of individuals verb**ally** to oppose or challenge police action without thereby risking arrest is one of the principal characteristics by which we distinguish a free nation from a police state." *Hill*, 482 U.S. at 463. Ideally, officers would not encounter verbal abuse. Communities would encourage mutual respect, and the police would likewise exhibit respect by treating people with dignity. But, particularly where officers engage in unconstitutional policing, they only exacerbate community opposition by quelling speech.

1. FPD Engages in a Pattern of Excessive Force in Violation of the Fourth Amendment

FPD engages in a pattern of excessive force in violation of the Fourth Amendment. Many officers are quick to escalate encounters with subjects they perceive to be disobeying their orders or resisting arrest. They have come to rely on ECWs, specifically Tasers®, where less force—or no force at all—would do. They also release canines on unarmed subjects unreasonably and before attempting to use force less likely to cause injury. Some incidents of excessive force result from stops or arrests that have no basis in law. Others are punitive and retaliatory. In addition, FPD records suggest a tendency to use unnecessary force against vulnerable groups such as people with mental health conditions or cognitive disabilities, and juvenile students. Furthermore, as discussed in greater detail in Part III.C. of this report, Ferguson's pattern of using excessive force disproportionately harms African-American members of the community. The overwhelming majority of force—almost 90%— is used against African Americans.

The use of excessive force by a law enforcement officer violates the Fourth Amendment. *Graham v. Connor*, 490 U.S. 386, 394 (1989); *Atkinson v. City of Mountain View, Mo.*, 709 F.3d 1201, 1207-09 (8th Cir. 2013). The constitutionality of an officer's use of force depends on whether the officer's conduct was "objectively reasonable' in light of the facts and circumstances," which must be assessed "from the perspective of a reasonable officer on the scene, rather than with the 20/20 vision of hindsight." *Graham*, 490 U.S. at 396. Relevant **consider**ations include "**the severity** of the crime at issue, whether the suspect poses an immediate threat to the safety of the officers, or others, and whether he is actively resisting arrest or attempting to evade arrest by flight." *Id.*; *Johnson v. Carroll*, 658 F.3d 819, 826 (8th Cir. 2011).

FPD also imposes limits on officers' use of force through department policies. The use-of-force policy instituted by Chief Jackson in 2010 states that "force may not be resorted to unless other reasonable alternatives have been exhausted or would clearly be ineffective under a particular set of circumstances." FPD General Order 410.01. The policy also sets out a use-of-force continuum, indicating the force options permitted in different circumstances, depending on the level of resistance provided by a suspect. FPD General Order 410.08.

FPD's stated practice is to maintain use-of-force investigation files for all situations in which officers use force. We reviewed the entire set of force files provided by the department for the period of January 1, 2010 to September 8, 2014. Setting aside the killing of animals (e.g., dogs, injured deer) and three instances in which the subject of the use of force was not identified, FPD provided 151 files. We also reviewed related documentation regarding canine deployments. Our finding that FPD force is routinely unreasonable and sometimes clearly punitive is drawn largely from FPD's documentation; that is, from officers' own words.

a. FPD's Use of Electronic Control Weapons Is Unreasonable

FPD's pattern of excessive force includes using ECWs in a manner that is unconstitutional, abusive, and unsafe. For example, in August 2010, a lieutenant used an ECW in drive-stun mode against an African-American woman in the Ferguson City Jail because she had refused to remove her bracelets. The lieutenant resorted to his ECW even though there were five officers present and the woman posed no physical threat.

Similarly, in November 2013, a correctional officer fired an ECW at an African-American woman's chest because she would not follow his verbal commands to walk toward a cell. The woman, who had been arrested for driving while intoxicated, had yelled an insulting remark at the officer, but her conduct amounted to verbal noncompliance or passive resistance at most. Instead of attempting hand controls or seeking assistance from a state trooper who was also present, the correctional officer deployed the ECW because the woman was "not doing as she was told." When another FPD officer wrote up the formal incident report, the reporting officer wrote that the woman "approached [the correctional officer] in a threatening manner." This "threatening manner" allegation appears nowhere in the statements of the correctional officer or witness trooper. The woman was charged with Disorderly Conduct, and the correctional officer soon went on to become an officer with another law enforcement agency.

These are not isolated incidents. In September 2012, an officer drive-stunned an African-American woman who he had placed in the back of his patrol car but who had stretched out her leg to block him from closing the door. The woman was in handcuffs. In May 2013, officers drivestunned a handcuffed African-American man who verbally refused to get out of the back seat of a police car once it had arrived at the jail. The man did not physically resist arrest or attempt to assault the officers. According to the man, he was also punched in the face and head. That allegation was neither reported by the involved officers nor investigated by their supervisor, who dismissed it. FPD officers seem to regard ECWs as an all-purpose tool bearing no risk. But an ECW—an electroshock weapon that disrupts a person's muscle control, causing involuntary contractions—can indeed be harmful. The Eighth Circuit Court of Appeals has observed that ECW-inflicted injuries are "sometimes severe and unexpected." *LaCross v. City of Duluth*, 713 F.3d 1155, 1158 (8th Cir. 2013). Electroshock "inflicts a painful and frightening blow, which temporarily paralyzes the large muscles of the body, rendering the victim helpless." *Hickey v. Reeder*, 12 F.3d 754, 757 (8th Cir. 1993). Guidance produced by the United States Department of Justice, Office of Community Oriented Policing Services, and the Police Executive Research Forum in 2011 warns that ECWs are "less lethal' and not 'nonlethal weapons'" and "have the potential to result in a fatal outcome." 2011 *Electronic Control Weapon Guidelines* 12 (Police Executive Research Forum & U.S. Dep't of Justice Office of Community Oriented Policing Services, Mar. 2011) ("2011 *ECW Guidelines*").

FPD officers' swift, at times automatic, resort to using ECWs against individuals who typically have committed low-level crimes and who pose no immediate threat violates the Constitution. As the Eighth Circuit held in 2011, an officer uses excessive force and violates clearly established Fourth Amendment law when he deploys an ECW against an individual whose crime was minor and who is not actively resisting, attempting to flee, or posing any imminent danger to others. *Brown v. City of Golden Valley*, 574 F.3d 491, 497-99 (8th Cir. 2011) (upholding the denial of a qualified immunity claim made by an officer who drive-stunned a woman on her arm for two or three seconds when she refused to hang up her phone despite being ordered to do so twice); cf. Hickey, 12 F.3d at 759 (finding that the use of a stun gun against a prisoner for refusing to sweep his cell violated the more deferential Eighth Amendment prohibition against cruel and unusual punishment). Courts have found that even when a suspect resists but does so only minimally, the surrounding factors may render the use of an ECW objectively unreasonable. *See Mattos v. Agarano*, 661 F.3d 433, 444-46, 448-51 (9th Cir. 2011) (en banc) (holding in two consolidated cases that minimal defensive resistance—including stiffening the body to inhibit being pulled from a car, and raising an arm in defense—does not render using an ECW reasonable where the offense was minor, the subject did not attempt to flee, and the subject posed no immediate threat to officers); *Parker v. Gerrish*, 547 F.3d 1, 9-11 (1st Cir. 2008) (upholding a jury verdict of excessive use of force for an ECW use because the evidence supported a finding that the subject who had held his hands together was not actively resisting or posing an immediate threat); *Casey v. City of Fed. Heights*, 509 F.3d 1278, 1282-83 (10th Cir. 2007) (holding that the use of an ECW was not objectively reasonable when the subject pulled away from the officer but did not otherwise actively resist arrest, attempt to flee, or pose an immediate threat).

Indeed, **of**ficers' unreasonable ECW use violates FPD's own policies. The department prohibits the use of force unless reasonable alternatives have been exhausted or would clearly be ineffective. FPD General Order 410.01. A separate ECW policy describes the weapon a **"design**ed to overcome active aggression or overt actions of assault." FPD General Order 499.00. The policy states that an ECW "will never be deployed punitively or for purposes of coercion. It is to be used as a way of averting a potentially injurious or dangerous situation." FPD General Order 499.04. Despite the existence of clearly established Fourth Amendment case law and explicit departmental policies in this area, FPD officers routinely engage in the unreasonable use of ECWs, and supervisors routinely approve their conduct.

It is in part FPD officers' approach to policing that leads them to violate the Constitution and FPD's own policies. Officers across the country encounter drunkenness, passive defiance, and verbal challenges. But in Ferguson, officers have not been trained or incentivized to use deescalation techniques to avoid or minimize force in these situations. Instead, they respond with impatience, frustration, and disproportionate force. FPD's weak **oversight** of officer use of force, described in greater detail below, facilitates this abuse. Officers should be required to view the ECW as one tool among many, and "a weapon of need, not a tool of convenience." 2011 ECW Guidelines at 11. Effective policing requires that officers not depend on ECWs, or any type of force, "at the expense of diminishing the fundamental skills of communicating with subjects and de-escalating tense encounters." Id. at 12.

b. FPD's Use of Canines on Low-level, Unarmed Offenders Is Unreasonable

FPD engages in a pattern of deploying canines to bite individuals when the articulated facts do not justify this significant use of force. The department's own records demonstrate that, as with other types of force, canine officers use dogs out of proportion to the threat posed by the people they encounter, leaving serious puncture wounds to nonviolent offenders, some of them children. Furthermore, in every canine bite incident for which racial information is available, the subject was African American. This disparity, in combination with the decision to deploy canines in circumstances with a seemingly low objective threat, suggests that race may play an impermissible role in officers' decisions to deploy canines.

FPD currently has four canines, each **assigned to** a particular canine officer. Under FPD policy, canines are to be used to locate and apprehend "dangerous offenders." FPD General Order 498.00. When offenders are hiding, the policy states, "handlers will not allow their K-9 to engage a suspect by biting if a lower level of force could reasonably be expected to control the suspect or allow for the apprehension." *Id.* at 498.06. The policy also permits the use of a canine, however, when any crime—not just a felony or violent crime—has been committed. Id. at 498.05. This permissiveness, combined with the absence of meaningful supervisory review and an apparent tendency to overstate the threat based on race, has resulted in avoidable dog bites to low-level offenders when other means of control were available.

In December 2011, officers deployed a canine to bite an unarmed 14-year-old African-American boy who was waiting in an abandoned house for his friends. Four officers, including a canine officer, responded to the house mid-morning after a caller reported that people had gone inside. Officers arrested one boy on the ground level. Describing the offense as a burglary in progress even though the facts showed that the only plausible offense was trespassing, the canine officer's report stated that the dog located a second boy hiding in a storage closet under the stairs in the basement. The officer peeked into the space and saw the boy, who was 5'5" and 140 pounds, curled up in a ball, hiding. According to the officer, the boy would not show his hands despite being warned that the officer would use the dog. The officer then deployed the dog, which bit the boy's arm, causing puncture wounds.

According to the boy, with whom we spoke, he never hid in a

storage space and he never heard any police warnings. He told us that he was waiting for his friends in the basement of the house, a vacant building where they would go when they skipped school. The boy approached the stairs when he heard footsteps on the upper level, thinking his friends had arrived. When he saw the dog at the top of the steps, he turned to run, but the dog quickly bit him on the ankle and then the thigh, causing him to fall to the floor. The dog was about to bite his face or neck but instead got his left arm, which the boy had raised to protect himself. FPD officers struck him while he was on the ground, one of them putting a boot on the side of his head. He recalled the officers laughing about the incident afterward.

The lack of sufficient documentation or a supervisory force investigation prevents us from resolving which version of events is more accurate. However, even if the officer's version of the force used were accurate, the use of the dog to bite the boy was unreasonable. Though described as a felony, the facts as described by the officer, and the boy, indicate that this was a trespass—kids hanging out in a vacant building. The officers had no factual predicate to believe the boy was armed. The offense reports document no attempt to glean useful information about the second boy from the first, who was quickly arrested. By the canine officer's own account, he saw the boy in the closet and thus had the opportunity to assess the threat posed by this 5'5" 14 year old. Moreover, there were no exigent circumstances requiring apprehension by dog bite. Four officers were present and had control of the scene.

There is a recurring pattern of officers claiming they had to use a canine to extract a suspect hiding in a closed space. The frequency with which **this particular** rationale is used to justify dog bites, alongside the conclusory language in the reports, provides cause for concern.

In December 2012, a 16-year-old African-American **b**oy suspected of stealing a ca**r** fled from **an** officer, jumpe**d** several fences, and ran into a vacant house. A second **of**ficer arrived with a canine, which reportedly located the suspect hiding in a closet. Without providing a warning outside the closet, the officer opened the door and sent in the dog, which bit the suspect and dragged him out by the legs. This force appears objectively unreasonable. *See Kuha v. City of Minnetonka*, 365 F.3d 590, 598 (8th Cir. 2004), abrogated on other grounds by *Szabla v. City of Brooklyn Park, Minn.*, 486 F.3d 385, 396 (8th Cir. 2007) (en banc) (holding that "a jury could find it objectively unreasonable to use a police dog trained in the bite and hold method without first giving the suspect a warning and opportunity for peaceful surrender"). The first officer, who was also on the scene by this point, deployed his ECW against the suspect three times as the suspect struggled with the dog, which was still biting him. The offense reports provide only minimal explanation for why apprehension by dog bite was necessary. The pursuing officer claimed the suspect had "reached into the front section of his waistband," but the report does not say that he relayed this information to the canine officer, and no weapon was found. Moreover, given the lack of a warning at the closet, the use of the dog and ECW at the same time, and the application of three ECW stuns in quick succession, the officers' conduct raises the possibility that the force was applied in retaliation for leading officers on a chase.

In November 2013, an officer deployed a canine to bite and detain a fleeing subject even though the officer knew the suspect was unarmed. The officer deemed the subject, an African American male who was walking down the street, suspicious because he appeared to walk away when he saw the officer. The officer stopped him and frisked him, finding no weapons. The officer then ran his name for warrants. When the man heard the dispatcher say over the police radio that he had outstanding warrants—the report does not specify whether the warrants were for failing to appear in municipal court or to pay owed fines, or something more serious—he ran. The officer followed him and released his dog, which bit the man on both arms. The officer's supervisor found the force justified because the officer released the dog "fearing that the subject was armed," even though the officer had already determined the man was unarmed.

As these incidents demonstrate, FPD officers' use of canines to bite people is frequently unreasonable. Officers command dogs to apprehend by biting even when multiple officers are present. They make no attempt to slow situations down, creating time to resolve the situation with lesser force. They appear to use canines not to counter a physical threat but to inflict punishment. They act as if every offender has a gun, justifying their decisions based on what might be possible rather than what the facts indicate is likely. Over**all**, FPD officers' use of canines reflects a culture in which officers choose not to use the skills and tactics that could resolve a situation without injuries, and instead deploy tools and methods that are almost guaranteed to produce an injury of some type.

FPD's use of canines is part of its pattern of excessive force in violation of the Fourth Amendment. In addition, FPD's use of dog bites only against African-American subjects is evidence of discriminatory policing in violation of the Fourteenth Amendment and other federal laws.

c. FPD's Use of Force Is Sometimes Retaliatory and Punitive

Many FPD uses of force appear entirely punitive. Officers often use force in response to behavior that may be annoying or distasteful but does not pose a threat. The punitive use of force by officers is unconstitutional and, in many cases, criminal. *See, e.g., Gibson v. County of Washoe, Nev.*, 290 F.3d 1175, 1197 (9th Cir. 2002) ("The Due Process clause protects pretrial detainees from the use of excessive force that amounts to punishment."); *see also* 18 U.S.C. § 242 (making willful deprivation of rights under color of law, such as by excessive force, a federal felony punishable by up to ten years in prison).

We r**evi**ewed many inci**den**ts in whi**c**h it appear**ed** that FPD officers used **for**ce not to counter a physical threat but to inflict punish**men**t. The use of canines and ECWs, in particular, appear prone to such abuse **by** FPD. In April 2013, for example, a correctional officer deployed an ECW against an African-

American prisoner, delivering a five-second shock, because the man had urinated out of his cell onto the jail floor. The correctional officer observed the man on his security camera feed inside the booking office. When the officer came out, some of the urine hit his pant leg and, he said, almost caused him to slip. "Due to the possibility of contagion," the correctional officer claimed, he deployed his ECW "to cease the assault." The ECW prongs, however, both struck the prisoner in **the** back. The correctional officer's claim that he deployed the ECW to stop the ongoing threat of urine is not credible, particularly given that the prisoner was in his locked cell with his back to the officer at the time the ECW was deployed. Using less-lethal force to counter urination, especially when done punitively as appears to be the case here, is unreasonable. *See Shumate v. Cleveland*, 483 F. App'x 112, 114 (6th Cir. 2012) (affirming denial of summary judgment on an excessive-force claim against an officer who punched a handcuffed arrestee in response to being spit on, when the officer could have protected himself from further spitting by putting the arrestee in the back of a patrol car and **closing** the door).

d. FPD Use of Force Often Results from Unlawful Arrest and Officer Escalation

A defining aspect of FPD's pattern of excessive force is the extent to which force results from unlawful stops and arrests, and from officer escalation of inci**d**ents. Too often, office**r**s overstep their authority by stopping individuals without reasonable suspicion and arresting without probable cause. Officers frequently compound the harm by using excessive force to effect the unlawful police action. Individuals encountering police under these circumstances are confused and surprised to find themselves being detained. They decline to stop or try to walk away, believing it within their rights to do so. They pull away incredulously, or respond with anger. Officers tend to respond to these reactions with force.

In January 2013, a patrol sergeant stopped an

African-American man after he saw the man talk to an individual in a truck and then walk away. The sergeant detained the man, although he did not articulate any reasonable suspicion that criminal activity was afoot. When the man declined to answer questions or submit to a frisk—which the sergeant sought to execute despite articulating no reason to believe the man was armed—the sergeant grabbed the man by the belt, drew his ECW, and ordered the man to comply. The man crossed his arms and objected that he had not done anything wrong. Video captured by the ECW's built-in camera shows that the man made no aggressive movement toward the officer. The sergeant fired the ECW, applying a five-second cycle of electricity and causing the man to fall to the ground. The sergeant almost immediately applied the ECW again, which he later justified in his report by claiming that the man tried to stand up. The video makes clear, however, that the man never tried to stand—he only writhed in pain on the ground. The video also shows that the sergeant applied the ECW nearly continuously for 20 seconds, longer than represented in his report. The man was charged with Failure to Comply and Resisting Arrest, but no independent criminal violation.

In a January 2014 incident, officers attempted to arrest a young African-American man for trespassing on his girlfriend's grandparents' property, even though the man had been invited into the home by the girlfriend. According to officers, he resisted arrest, requiring several officers to subdue him. Seven officers repeatedly struck and used their ECWs against the subject, who was 5'8" and 170 pounds. The young man suffered head lacerations with significant bleeding.

In the above examples, force resulted from temporary detentions or attempted arrests for which officers lacked legal authority. Force at times appeared to be used as punishment for noncompliance with an order that lacked legal authority. Even where FPD officers have legal grounds to stop or arrest, however, they frequently take actions that ratchet up tensions and needlessly escalate the situation to the point that they feel force is necessary. One illustrative instance from October 2012 began as a purported check on a pedestrian's well-being and ended with the man being taken to the ground, drive-stunned twice, and arrested for Manner of Walking in Roadway and Failure to Comply. In that case, an African-American man was walking after midnight in the outer lane of West Florissant Avenue when an officer asked him to stop. The officer reported that he believed the man might be under the influence of an "impairing substance." When the man, who was 5'7" and 135 pounds, kept walking, the officer grabbed his arm; when the man pulled away, the officer forced him to the ground. Then, for reasons not articulated in the officer's report, the officer decided to handcuff the man, applying his ECW in drive-stun mode twice, reportedly because the man would not provide his hand for cuffing. The man was arrested but there is no indication in the report that he was in fact impaired or indeed doing anything other than walking down the street when approached by the officer.

In November 2011, officers stopped a car for speeding. The two African-American women inside exited the car and vocally objected to the stop. They were told to get back in the car. When the woman in the passenger seat got out a second time, an officer announced she was under arrest for Failure to Comply. This decision escalated into a use of force. According to the officers, the woman swung her arms and legs, although apparently not at anyone, and then stiffened her body. An officer responded by drive-stunning her in the leg. The woman was charged with Failure to Comply and Resisting Arrest.

As these examples demonstrate, a significant number of the documented use-of-force incidents involve charges of Failure to Comply and Resisting Arrest only. This means that officers who claim to act based on reasonable suspicion or probable cause of a crime either are wrong much of the time or do not have an adequate legal basis for many stops and arrests in the first place

Highly Commended Poems

Jason Allen-Paisant

On Property

I

A white woman is walking her dog in Central Park   The dog is off its leash
though signs say dogs must be leashed at all times   A black man asks her to
   leash her dog

    An African American man

She is   confused and afraid

   even in violation
of the rules
    I have authority over this space and   you

The woman shouts at the man   the man films the scene   the woman shouts
   even more

I am going to tell them
an African American man
is threatening my life

repeats this line to operator

She has lost control of her voice
is shrieking   with fear
even as she clutches thrashing dog

She is   confused and afraid

       The   *African American*
       the space
       the violation
       The *African American*
       man

How ordinary for her
to destroy

this body
How ordinary for her

to erase
this body
space

On this day
Floyd is also dying
with a foot on his neck
exhaling
his last breath on concrete
calling for Mama

II

He does not forget this
The park too is a death zone
            ancient

he puts on his glasses
            he's going out
            of place

he hopes
to soften his look of threatening   he hopes
that as he walks this way

those little round
  nerdy
            eye-
            glasses

will make him small   enough
to those vulnerable to this
type of body

perhaps it's the eyes
    the eyes not seen too much

III

He goes into
          the woods
with desire

he hears birdcalls
          he remembers

the park too
is a death zone

he does not
forget this
                    ancient

what the park is

Threa Almontaser

And That Fast, You're Thinking about Their Bodies

At a rooftop party, you dance near every edge. Someone drops a ring in glass, in your head the clink of a used bullet, still hot, and that fast the rooftop is covered with wires, riflemen, and you're thinking about mutiny, Mk47s, two cities clawing at each other's bruised throats while boys try to hold your hips, keep dancing. The war is on your hips. Your hands. You wear it all over. You wrap your hair in it. Pluck it from your eyebrows. The rooftop is wide and caring, too rained or sometimes incensed, and you never once think to be afraid of what could arrow a cloud and kill it. You eat volcano rolls, pink pepper goat cheese, and the war enters you. You stare at *Still Life with Flowers and Fruit* and the glade of roses scream war. Here with a doctor and your pregnant aunt who hasn't yet learned English, only speaks in war. Friends in Greensboro get picked up by bored police, get beat up for no reason, and those fists carry war. Job interviews, you carve yourself into a white-known shape and that renaming is a kind of war. You take a passport photo, told to smile without teeth, the flash a bright war. You're on the other side of mercy with your meadows and fluffed spillage, where nights are creamed with saviors. Here everyone rests on roofs graduated and sung, gazing at a sky that won't bleed them. At the beach, you're buried to the neck, practicing dead, snug in your chosen tomb, gulls flittering on all sides, waves fleshing closer, and that fast, you're thinking of a grubby desert girl who placed small stones in her scarf, shook it back and forth, said, *This is what the sea must sound like.*

Tiffany Atkinson

Clean windows

Sean   the new department manager
spends all the petty cash
on window cleaners
for these huge panes
six floors up

They all have their foibles
says Pinky   shucking a glove
with a smack   We're in
the main ward   high and formal
as an Oxbridge hall

A trolley turns a corner
somewhere deep and then
as if the hospital
swings downwind
and hangs on its anchor

calm rolls up the jinxy
stairwells to this floor   where
through the hand-rinsed glass
we watch a white van
climb out of the valley

to the new world   What's
a word for how the light
this cold May afternoon
ruffles the blue pleated curtain
behind Mr Mooney

reaching for his tumbler
like a man underwater? I
have   *lumen*   biro'd on my hand

because the nurse who used it
scuttled off before I got to ask

What's a lumen   Pinky?
Just an opening   she says

Khairani Barokka

in which i hypnotise a tiger

not made for blake quotes and tinder profiles.
not squandered for bullets slung as attempts
at gumption. not slit with knives on colonists'
orders, then strung up. not sold to a venture
capitalist who'll place her pale feet in heels
and on you. not vanishing. not a chipmunk-
cheeked emoji. not bedtime threat to children
in cold climates. not CGI recreation with an
underappreciated actor voicing you. not a
bevy of ill-advised tattoos. not *the hangover*.
not sports team embodiment. not go get 'em.
not taxidermy. not species forgotten. not a
name used for foreplay. not a fantastic form
of balm for soothing creaking muscle tissue.
not a totem for my calming alone. not tired
and misunderstood and hiding and rotting
and gone. scream without shame or fear of
banishment. this is no forest of wounding,
tribulation, dust of your bone. lick your paws.

                    open your eyes.

Alex Bell

Arkteia

There are songs that have you in them like a pit.
Stubborn and rock-salt, sick with romantic delusions.
I'd like to tell you some recent discoveries –
that Fanny Blankers Cohen won four gold medals
aged thirty with two children; that there are wild monkeys in Gibraltar.
They called her the flying housewife. It's indeed not enough
to watch each morning come and think *tomorrow*
because it is too hard to see you die. Gundog, hound, utility,
terrier, working, pastoral, toy. Fray Bentos is a port city in Uruguay.
At the sanctuary of Artemis in Brauron, young girls dressed as bears –
devout, baskets of figs in their hands, dancing the heavy steps of bears.

Leo Boix

Meditations of An Immigrant (Cinquaines)

Upstairs
a bus to Deal
I'll beat the hell out of
you heard the Kentish lad. Scratched panes
fog up

*

Angler
on a bulked pier.
He wears waterproof shorts.
Out with the bloody immigrants,
the lot

*

There was
a well so deep
where all the coins were thrown
a stone block where they gathered, cut
some throats

*

Sleep tight
for night is all
there is: the limbs of men
their pain and grief. I too succumb
to this

*

On Earth
not much to see:
a road, few pilgrims, wars . . .
Books rare, but then people could read
the stars

Elizabeth-Jane Burnett

Barrel Jellyfish

> 'The [US] administration has taken a hatchet to climate change language across government websites … mentions of climate change have been excised, buried or stripped of any importance'
> The *Guardian*, 14th May, 2017

To be a risky thing, run in water thing, early riser.

As a robin, as a jaybird, as an eye. We put our parts together. We outward

form. We resemble. As rusks, as plants grow in marshy ground, as wind. We be longing to peril, in press of pressing on. If we disappear

try us with different titles.

Say we were frost or fruit. Say we were whale fat. Say we were good for the economy, or don't say anything.

Plait a rope, thread a hundred of our mouths together, let only sea unravel us.

Look for us, even after we are gone. With eight arms there's a chance one may keep, wrongly filed under

weapons.

Dom Bury

The Opened Field

Six boys, a calf's tongue each, one task —
to gulp each slick muscle down in turn,
to swallow each vein whole and not give
back a word, a sign, our mothers' names.
The scab stripped off, the ritual learned —
five boys step out across an empty field.

Five boys step out across an empty field
to find a fire already made, the task
to dock then brand a single lamb. We learnt
fast how to hold, then cut, then turn
each tail away, to print in it our names —
our ownership. We dock, we brand, give

iron to the skin until at last their legs give.
Four boys step out across an empty field,
each small child waiting for a name,
our own name to be called, the next task
ours to own, ours to slice into, to turn
each blade, to shear off skin until we learnt

the weight of it. One by one we learnt
the force our bodies hold, the subtle give
our own hands have, how not to turn
our gaze. Three boys stand in a frozen field —
each child stripped and hosed, the next task
not to read the wind but learn the names

we have for snow, each term, each name
we have given to the world. To then unlearn
ourselves, the self, this is — the hardest task.
To have nothing left. No thing but heat to give.
Two boys step out across an empty field.
Still waiting for the call, waiting for our turn,

waiting to become, to dig, to turn
at last our hands into the soil then name
the weakest as an offering — the field
opened to a grave, my last chore not to learn
the ground but taste it closed. I don't give
back a word, surprised I am the task —

that what the land gives it must then learn
to turn back into soil. One child, a name its task
to steal. Five boys turn from an empty field.

Lewis Buxton

Taxidermy

The girl at the party holds aloft her stuffed capuchin
and explains how you cut straight down the middle, suck
out the organs, like a foot coming out of a sock of skin,

then you stitch it back together. The brain, you dry up
with a chemical so it won't rot. Former Mr California
Rich Piana, collapsed at 45 whilst having a haircut.

At the autopsy they found his heart & liver
were twice the weight of a regular man's. They sliced
into him, opened his sternum to see and I wonder

if they thought of stuffing him? Freezing his blue-white
eyes & bleached grin, putting his body on show
looking more real than he ever did in life.

Anne Carson

Sure, I Was Loved

for Dimitris Papaioannou

I tame you.
(No you don't.)
You were nude.
You were intangible.
You were unconvincing.
You were vague.
You claimed you were born from angels.
You stank of the horrors of war.
You blazed with ruthless pride.
Your full, loose mouth blazed.
You had a fruit bloom.
You bloomed like a cannibal.
Ready to devour or be devoured.
Or both.
You had your portrait painted as a butcher's block.
Yet you were not a still life.
You were meat but recently living.
You had come with your own legs.
I replaced your legs.
I replaced your crotch.
Crotches.
All of them.
You were ghosting around as if a mystery of Hymen.
I undressed you.
That is the only difference.
Beyond that there was little development between us.
I used crutches, stilts, evisceration, plaster casts.
I rooted your shoes.
I tilted the stage, I knocked it apart, I combined you with other
    genders.
I rolled up my sleeves.

I showed you no tenderness, we might as well have been sexual!
Or medical!
Or archaeologists!
I required you to clean up whatever mess we made.
I used the mess again next day.
I slowed your steps, inhibited your breathing, assaulted you with
    film score music (waltz).
I littered the stage with open graves and you fell into them –
    hilarious!
I laughed at you!
I made you walk on your hands without oxygen or effective friends.
I made you build the floor you walked on.
I blew your clothes off.
I mangled your Orpheus scene.
I threw someone else's thighs at you.
I doused you with the waters of Lethe.
I flattened you into a lozenge and stuffed you in my pocket.
I shot all the arrows of King Darius' Persian army at you (fast!)
then made you pick them all up (slow).
I tossed your skeleton off its slab (it smashed).
I played with your skull.
I got you chasing a nostalgic scrap of paper then turned out the
    lights
and told the audience to go home.
Beyond that nothing was resolved between us.
The legs were of various heights.
You invited me into your golden age, I made you a stranger,
a loser, an arriviste, an undocumented alien, an unclaimed hostage,
a bad birthday gift.
I had you eaten into by the human.
I broke your energy,
I invented your gravity,
I pulled you out through your own peep-hole.
(No you didn't.)
I tame you.
(No you don't.)

Sumita Chakraborty

O Spirit

Of Moby-Dick

I wish to lay before you
a particular, plain statement
whose skeleton we are
briefly to exhibit
out of the trunk,
the branches grow, out of them,
the twigs
chased over the watery
moors, slaughtered
in the valleys—oil and bone
pass unscathed through the fire
and it is only
gray imperfect misty dawn,
soon we shall be lost
in its unshored, harborless
immensities that serene
ocean rolled eastwards from me
a thousand leagues of blue and I only
am escaped alone to tell thee
only I am escaped to tell thee.

John Challis

The Last Good Market

Being faithless, I've always preferred to think of death
as the end of a movie, no sequels
or questions, the final scene as clear as glass,
no room for misinterpretation or for reading into
by sceptical scholars; this one's for the pragmatists
who like to know the end before it starts.

But watching Eileen on the day that we cremated Fred
had me thinking of a compromise, how after all there might be
somewhere they all congregate, worn out
from the journey across the barren afterlife.
Take your pick: the golden city,
the courtyard made of cloud, or the house

that you were born in. Though I can't shake
the feeling that nurses rouse to empty wards
with no one but themselves to heal, and from blackboards
teachers turn to classrooms of abandoned chairs and desks,
and that one day my father will wake up from snoring
in his black cab to wait for no fares on the rank.

But there are those of us who like our work,
and glad again to be of use, Fred is lifting up
the muddied sacks in the last good market,
admiring how his muscles flex, to fill the stall
with growth as fresh as the January morning
when he slipped out of his suffering and beyond

the fruitless task of dreaming up the ways
that faith employs the dead. I know that we must let them rest.
But I'm compelled to speak of what at night they show me:
the streets where they hold daily market,
where they shout their throats red-raw
and serve their last deductions on imperishable goods.

Suzanne Cleary

For the Poet Who Writes to Me While Standing in Line at CVS, Waiting for His Mother's Prescription

for Russell Jackson

It's nothing that you flat out say, Russell, but your email
reminds me that six months into pandemic, five months
into quarantine, CVS remains open 24 hours, its harsh
blue-white light steady, as nothing in nature is steady,

those long fluorescent bulbs still dive-bombing lumens
so that midnight is bright as 8 a.m., or 4 a.m., or 2 p.m.,
or 7:30 p.m. You can see that I struggle to carry
one thought to the next, these long days. I spend hours

on the Internet, becoming expert on the height of actors
from Hollywood's Golden Age, on the 25 Cutest Photos
of four-year-old Princess Charlotte. I now know
that Elizabeth Bishop was a bit taller than I am,

a bit heavier. Her clothes would be too big for me,
as no doubt her shoes. Russell, what is it that supposedly
concentrates the mind wonderfully? Samuel Johnson said it,
in Boswell's biography,which I have never read and never

will. I know my limits. Lately, I think that I know little else
worth knowing. My only advice for your poems, Russell:
wash your hands for as long as it takes to sing 'Happy Birthday'.
Did you know that's no longer copyrighted? Five years ago,

US District Court Judge George H. King ruled
'Happy Birthday' is Public Domain, the 1935 patent applied
only to the melody and specific arrangements of the tune,
but not to the actual song itself. When Judge King writes

actual song, he means lyrics, but I hear him saying
song is something beyond the reach of law, beyond reach
of language. Song is like a kernel of light, inside of things,
steady. Russell, be like CVS. I don't know what this means,

be like CVS. Russell, dare to say what doesn't make sense,
then wait patiently to see the sense inside of it. Be like CVS.
Be like the bewildering variety of toothpastes, decongestants,
hair conditioners. Be like orange Velcro knee braces,

like spools of pastel ribbon that hums, pulled across a scissors.
Be like the aisle of bare shelves where the cleaning products stood,
where the white metal shelves now display only how each shelf,
with a simple ingenious hook, fits into the frame.

I'm telling you nothing that you don't already know, Russell.
Be like whatever accepts the horrid light, and shines in it.
Be like the 8-ounce can of lightly salted cashews, for which
you are newly willing to pay $12.99, as you stand in line

waiting for the blue-gloved hands to hold out to you
the small white bag, which is not for you,
except in that you are the one
who will carry it where it must go.

David Constantine

Jimmy Knight

Waking this morning I remembered Jimmy Knight
From Hope Road Primary School. Every kid could tell
What sort of a family life every other kid had
By how they were shod and clad and fed
And whether they looked you in the eyes all right
And smiled or never did and by their smell.

Jimmy had none of the good signs and all of the bad.
I remember his scared white face, the snot
And elsewhere of him that was damp. But one
Last lesson of the afternoon, all the lights were on
Smog at the windows, in her normal voice Mrs Thomas said
Come out the front, Jimmy, love, and sing to us

And doing as he was told that's what he did
Came out the front and wiped his nose on his jersey sleeve
Covered the wet with his hands and lifted up his eyes
Towards something he could see and we could not
And sang us 'Somewhere over the Rainbow'
But without the words if I recall it right or none

We understood though a blackbird might for all I know
Or the angels I suppose, pure melody it was
Pure carolling, the breath of clearness, always near
Or perhaps already gone beyond a world of tears
Clean lovely it soared and dipped and soared again
It was grace, what he'd had given him not asking why, he gave

Till he stopped and returned from wherever he'd been
Stood still, eyes down, in the silence, and Mrs Thomas said
Thank you, Jimmy, love, and the small soiled lad
Went back to his place and looked the same
And outside was the smog that dripped from the skies
And left black on the masks we wore to school and home.

Polina Cosgrave

My People

My people love to eat
the black apples of victory.
They fall from tall bony trees
like bombs in the night
leaving cracks in the yellow soil.
They lie around, these juicy mines.
That's when my people crawl on their bellies
to gather them into their helmets.
Filled with blood, ashes and gunpowder,
black apples explode in our mouths
like fireworks on Victory Day
tearing our intestines to shreds.
So we march with pride for
our city
our war
our dead.
My people dig up another hundred unknown soldiers.
We will never run out of them.
As long as we have our apple trees
planted by the victors
we will dig to find the inflamed roots.
Each time I eat a black apple
I smile like I still have a head.

Maia Elsner

After Auden's 'Musée des Beaux Arts'

i

Published in 1940   *something amazing*   already
Poland ravaged   & the poet walks *dully along*   Renata taken
Cecilia taken   amid all of this –   Janek
(where is Janek?)   the gypsies on the plains   annihilated & meanwhile
Auden focusses on a   painting of   an expensive
delicate ship   passing   *not an important failure*
the people on the shore busy   ignoring   the splash
the ploughman   not recognizing   a boy falling out
the sky   legs disappearing   feathers into foam
(where is Janek?)   reduced to   ekphrasis
the politician talks about   statistics while   reporters film drowning

The way we plough   *through life*   in 'Icarus
Again'   writes Devenish   *you'd think*
we'd have enough   *of falling*   enough of myth &
theory   particularly   Eurocentric vision
how long will Greek be   (assumed) universal   Kantaris says
the whole Aegean   *not wide enough*   *to hold the impact*
of death. Today   Icarus   is a refugee
dumped   along the journey   *because tragedies happen*
Icarus is   everything   you want her to be
a *civil war*   *slays* her, says Coleman   loose as feathers
fallen woman   made metaphor   through history

Martina Evans

Hackney Trident

I think of Liam when I stand on a chair, shaking
as I should have been, considering what I found out afterwards –
that the fuse box didn't work. The current was
running two ways in a loop –
I think that was what the fourth electrician said.

It didn't trip for twenty years and I'd been worried
all that time if I'd remember how to wind the wire if it did trip
which it couldn't.

Liam's all you can afford, Martina, John was laughing.
He said the same about Spud Murph and
the amorous plumber.

Liam was very shook inside his too-big grey trousers, his legs
bending like ashplants, his grey stubble, the metallic sweet
smell of last night's alcohol,
hands trembling on the fixtures.

Will he take a cheque? *Jesus, if you offered Liam a cheque
he'd cry,* all of them squeezed into the van, waiting
for me to fork out so they could go.

He's all you can afford, Martina.

After Liam, the devout Catholic electrician's white eyebrows were
leaping,

*Did you know that washing machine had no earth? It's a disgrace for
any man to leave it that way
in a house with young girls.*

What about boys, middle-aged and old people?

And that thing!

The Hackney Trident, our 1920s cut-out
with its Jules Verne look and a habit of humming – a zzzzzzsssing
so I didn't go down to it much.

When the devout Catholic died, his hitherto quiet side-kick
son turned up flaming drunk at 8.a.m.
All right. All right. I know what I'm doing!

Mick from UK Power Direct took it away in the end.
He said the Trident could be *very classy*, but he didn't
say my rusty, paint-splashed one was
although I still have a piece of its porcelain.

His parents were from Mayo and Kerry but he didn't say that
until we were alone.

I was lucky to have a Trident. If I was on
the other side of the road, I'd have
one of the Islington ones.

We don't tell people we call them
Islington Deathboxes. You can't work on them live –
everything has to be off.

And we didn't even have an earth, the old one
had rusted away back to Mother Earth.
Mick drilled a new one down.

The last time I tried John, he wasn't laughing.
He'd gone to collect Liam from his flat,
The man was cold in his bed. John, already
scared by his exploding oesophageal varices.

I'd say he was there a while, Martina.

Kit Fan

Suddenly

Never use 'suddenly', the most overused, least-needed
word in fiction.
                    Elmore Leonard

Suddenly, the cloud-knots unravelled and a droplet fell
from a womb. Three days of hard labour had broken
her. She said she was too tired to name the boy.

Suddenly, the blackened milk teeth gave up after a year
of antibiotics. The doctors baffled. His locked mouth was fed
swifts' solidified saliva to clear his feverish chest.

Home left him suddenly.

At a zebra crossing, his father suddenly took his hand.
No cars, no danger ahead, but being held was a strange thing.
Moving in with his family, stranger.

Suddenly, he stopped speaking first week at school.
Teacher called his mother in. When asked to explain
the silence, he said he had nothing to say.

Suddenly at 14, on a bridge, he vowed never to reproduce.

Desire suddenly overtook fear. After watching
Kieślowski's *Dekalog* in one sitting he spelt out his heart
and asked what togetherness meant. Joe walked off in the rain.

Years later, suddenly, he discovered from the *Book of Not*:
not watching *Dekalog*, not asking the right question,
not spelling things out, no Joe and no rain.

Suddenly, a handful of milk-seeds, and suddenly, men …

Suddenly 2001. Two professors persuaded him
to study a malleable thing called literature.
Hong Kong had returned to China but he flew to Britain.

Suddenly, people spoke Yorkshire. Luv on the bus.
Luv in the shops. Yorkshire stared at him and he stared
back, like two neurons in a busy translation loop.

Suddenly, one autumn, he found love and blockades.

A log-jam and suddenly diversions. Everywhere the road
signs read Divorce, Teenagers, Anorexia. He claimed driving
was in his DNA because his father was a taxi driver.

Suddenly, his tongue tripped on the English alphabet
when he rebuilt Telford Gardens Library he was brought up in
but now demolished. People called that poetry.

Suddenly, a voice, a temporary abode.

Suddenly he failed, and blamed the words
and the swifts' saliva. How many edible bird nests were robbed
in exchange for a lottery of half-tuned stolen keys?

And what could he say to the superior blast
that suddenly erased his vocal cords, retinas, eardrums, taste buds,
and all the tensions on his fingertips, tendons, heart?

Suddenly, rain churns up the clouds. And, stops.

Joseph Fasano

Letter to Lorca Written on His Piano, Granada, 2019

An ocean away, my country is dying.

Traveler,
I have had to touch
these dark keys
of your shadow

to know we feel our griefs
ahead of us
with their cargo

like great ships passing in the darkness
as we wade out, naked, through the shallows.

I have had to ask my own ghosts
where they go.

Come, you say,
come with me
awhile.

If the heart
is a dark horse on the roadway,
you can follow it

with its black tack
and its saddle,

follow it
in the mad hands of its captors,
dark bread loaded on its shoulders.

You can listen to the last good songs of earth.

Listen: it is late now.
It is later.

I have touched the maddened jasmine
in your garden;
I have smoothed the sheets
you rumpled when they took you;

I have lain down
in your linens
nothing burned.

Go, then. It is late.
The world is burning.

Córdoba,
Santaella,
Ángel—

And when they knelt you
in the new moon
on that lost road,

when your body
was a country that couldn't love you,

did you look up
at the dark stars in their gardens
and hear the night air, the silences, the wind's hands?

I had wanted, love,
to leave this
in the wind's hands,

but I hear you, now,

I hear you
now, I do:

Go, now. Your life waits
on the roadway.
Walk it back
through the dark sleep of its captors.

Love someone like the last song of the world.

Annie Freud

Rimbaud's Ovaries – A Mondegreen for Our Times

For Jon Sayers

Birds move abroad. Sad armies raid armoires.
Suave Eros daubs a morbid vase, admires ordure,
bids a rose adieu.

Murder sires murder, buries Aubade's muse.
A dossier – massive, abrasive, biased –
arrives. Boum.

Odium's rude brass marauds our ears.
Bravado rams demur aside. Idioms
embarrass us.

A rabid virus devours a biomass
as Ovid's rubied rivieras void bruised bodies
overboard. Ossaria brim.

Note

The etymology of the mondegreen:

In a 1954 essay in *Harper's* magazine, the American writer
Sylvia Wright described how, as a young girl, she misheard the
line from the ballad 'The Bonnie Earl of Moray', 'and laid him on
the green' as 'and Lady Mondegreen'. Wright explains the need
for a new term, as follows: *The point about what I shall hereafter call*
mondegreens, is that they are better than the original.

Angela Gardner

Shoddy Tarnished Gifts

No-one but us, on an empty horizon.
We are thrown into a terrible wilderness.
Our shredded shirt sail lolls in its open window
of sky (filthy old rags) above paths
of the sea unmade and purposeless.

Another day, the sun a howling mouth
our lips a wasteland. Unable to speak
throats filled with stones, tongues swollen
in our mouths. Lips black and cracked
limbs gross and becoming useless.

The shoddy, tarnished gifts of shiny
mottled skin taut with iron barbs, tight
and seared with pain.

Alan Gillis

The Readiness

It could happen at sunset
on a sloping lawn.
In a yawning estate
it could happen at dawn.

In a queue for your therapist,
in the public baths,
on a road through the forest
it could happen in a flash.

Under a harvest moon,
in a lift, on the stairs,
in an encrypted chatroom:
it could happen anywhere.

So make sure you're up to speed
when, at sunset or dawn,
worms vex the seed,
crows shadow the corn.

Jen Hadfield

Dolmen

Standing stone, let's
talk about
You! Who knows
how deep this grief goes
down – in your thick waist
and whalebone skirt –
      goodnessknows
how deep and wide –
twinkling modestly with
garnet, feldspar –

whiffing
(faintly) of bruised
mushroom.

Now, we learnt in
school about Deep
Time. Six

o'clock shadow: lichen.
Pouringdownlikeporridge:
lichen. But humankind
are brief, soft

fireworks, prone
to go off at a moment's
notice. Are we even speaking the
same language? Urgently

we hammer at your
boarded-up window,
      rattle and try

your grittygrey door!

Maryam Hessavi

Red Cities

I came to this planet earth
with cherries hanging on my ears

and I was not a girl.
I am also that girl.

I followed the path of the horse's gallop,
by a setar that played without strings

and I was not a musician. I am
also that hand that plays. The man

dropped a coin for my sound.
I am that man. The glint rolled as sound

loaded a horn so loud it banged
and worth was fashioned well. I am

a bursted eardrum. The ear felt
wind sigh past. Wind cuts across

the ear. That ear is me.
The ear is a house that rests

on water with stilts that wobble.
Those stilts are me. And that house

belongs to me. Mine is my name
and my body. The body is

me   where no maps are drawn.
The pencil belongs to me. I am

the belonger, and he is mine and me. Mine
is a home of cherry trees and they are

sharpened. I am the stone from one
eaten. That meal is me and I kneel

before the mouth that does.
Teeth are me. Gums.

The tongue is enough.
I am taste buds and they

flower an orchard every June.
I am June. My Mother is Joon.

Joon is a place over bitter seas.
I am that. I do not sail past blue lines.

joon, meaning 'dear' in Farsi

Victoria Kennefick

Beached Whale

At first I thought that enormous lump of red-brown on the sand
was the trunk of some ancient, washed-up tree.

It was only when I mounted the object,
digging my small hands into something far too pliable,
that it really hit me, the stale smell of a thousand low tides

and the mute open mouths of the many onlookers
with their hysterical dogs, the seagulls circling like squalling clouds,
my mother's curlew scream as she ran towards me, disjointed.

Astride the whale like this,
looking at my mother move through dimensions,
planes of distance,

I thought of boutique dressing rooms brimming
with clothes and tension, like gas, expanding. And of two little girls
watching their mother cry at her reflection distorted in a
    fluorescent mirror.

The weight of her past made flesh on her hips,
the scars of our arrivals barely healed after all this time,
my blind hands all over the body.

Grasping, desperate to hold onto something real,
not knowing what that was.

Fran Lock

La jena di Londra

that the red-eyed hyena, padding dust on a trail,
has a conscience that swings between zero and nil
                                                    Roddy Lumsden

but perhaps you are mistaken. *this* meat – inscrutable
ruby salvo – is for you. for all things trounced, and then
devoured. the high-wire stretched from mayhem to
amends. the bluesy prowl between whiskey promise,
smouldering ploy. the gonzo ballads of your friends.
la dolce morte. such sultry treatment from a reckless
girl, her tenement treacle's quicksand sought. but she
preferred those jesting boys to the rheumy diamonds
you had bought. for every gaffe and every chance, for
every straying article of fate. for skipping needles,
quibbled luck; the bruising taste of szechuan pork, for
every baroque marinade that did you wrong. *this* meat
is for you. there's sympathetic magic in a smacked lip.
the saints may lisp their miracles, the lilies wilt,
the truculent young forget. but hyena is here, in her
fatalist's mane, her coif of thorns, and bringing offals
red, and soft, and wet enough to cleanse. be sated. sit.
as if never a grim shilling bent in the slot, or the brazen
ablutions of suicide; no craquelure of night or mind, no
stinging shot of glycerite, when all you need's the inky
sluice of cassis or kahlúa. no mirthless slur. no lank
malarial hour of woe, and you, standing matador
before the night bus, sow your brassy hymns in
the a.m.'s meanest acre. hyena is here, will race her
russet flex to dust. brings scent of musky meadow
gasp; a fitful eccentricity of sky. *this* meat sees you
pirouette, and dive. some kelpy morning with
the wind in your teeth, and far from here. no *book*
of going forth by day. and far from here. to sway

upon some flinty scarp, tarrying and vandal. this
awful city has no natives. numbing strangeness'
suck. but *this* i caught in open fields. i carried it
home for you, dear heart, eat, deer heart, be
resolute and wild.

lisa luxx

for a subculture to resist capitalist co-opting it must remain impossible to define

Dyke is not my sexuality* dyke is my gender: the She that exists outside the male gaze. The earth is a dyke, if you held her in bed you'd sink into the softness of her skin and she'd flex her bicep in response, knowing gold you are forbidden to mine for. Dyke is my political party, I've seen a city in rubble and watched butches and femmes knot hairs and carry whole neighbourhoods beneath the paving stones while gay boys bowed and made their speeches. Dyke is my street fighter of choice, the way I square my shoulders when I mean 'listen', dyke is the way I listen. Dyke is how I accessorise with bite marks but would marry the cradle. Dyke is the splinters and snags in my fingers from chopping wood, dyke is how I'll always keep you warm. There is a religion to dyke, a belief in the bond and bind in the women and non-binary kind who choir eternal and pulse in formation. Dyke is every no we spell with possibility, every rapture made with mouth shields and dew. Dyke the lucky strike, dyke the uncontainable, dyke the symbol that fails in order to succeed. They invented guns when they couldn't catch birds, dyke is still the ungrabbable wing. Dyke is both my nerves and my steel, dyke moon in water, dyke sun chiselling clouds to let tension out. I learnt to hold my breath, which trained me to submarine into the deepest bonds where we pass in-jokes and lightning bolts between us. Dyke the comrade, dyke the harvest, guardian o friend! Among bike chains and clippers, horoscopes and crystals, with the blessed and the butch, my god we feel true. Come now, every, b-o-i, stud, bad bitch and honey,   you are a horizon.

* My sexuality is Men Don't Deserve Me.

Gail McConnell

'The Clouded Border I like best'

The Clouded Border I like best
it's like a cow on wings I saw one
by the lough shore where we ate
our picnic black and white in
patches ink spills on a tissue
that's another one The Tissue
Moth I've never seen except one
held on pins look at the
underside our teacher says our
fingers on the glass the
butterflies live under only they
don't live by The Speckled Wood
I spy The Gatekeeper
The Forester by them The Ghost
Moth and The Silver Y

Andrew McMillan

pill-box

before   I'd only ever seen them at my grandparents'
each day piled high with coloured tablets the size
of my little finger   each morning's handful
a way of distracting the body from its decline
so when your mind wouldn't settle   and you couldn't
remember   we got one too   a little plastic calendar
in the kitchen   at first you hated it
felt it drew too much attention to itself
like an errant child   but eventually
it left the cupboard for the corner of the worktop
where each night it would sit ready   like a packed lunch
and it felt like recovery   a series
of small windows to be opened   to scoop out
brief comfort   until one day you thought it too big
too obvious   and we dug out my grandad's from the deep
of some forgotten box   small   flesh-pink
each day like opening a knuckle on a fist
and inside the white static of all the powdered years
his blood pressure   his heart   and I think we mistook it for love
this closed hand of a pill-box   skinny as a child's wrist
that things are easier to live with if you think
they're smaller   just one mouthful   open wide

Alexandra Melville

Hippo

Go on, you say, and hand me up the ladder, balanced
awkwardly in my tutu like some balletic hippo out of *Fantasia*,
which probably you never saw. Father told me, at the cinema
when he was six, the mouse magician scared the shit out of him.
Before my mother, he smoked Gauloises coolly on a mountain top.
People change. You're not wearing your top hat, so I don't know
if this is real or just a rehearsal. Behind us there is a dark forest
and sometimes a yellow veld, trees parasoled flat in the heat.
If I turn for a clear look, the sceneshifter drives it off in his truck.

Get in. The box is somewhat longer than my body, like a coffin
lined with white lace. Some wag has littered it with confetti.
It takes a certain mind to lie in a coffin and stay still. The box
is in three parts, painted with scenes and symbols: the pride
of lions, the murders of crows, two rings, a constant moon.
There are parallel slots along the sides. I know what they are for.
This is where you'll plunge in the swords. These blades are real –
someone in the crowd has tested the steel bite against their tongue.
There is space for an axe between each joined segment of the box.

You will help me into this strange bed in my white dress and roses.
You'll smooth the hair from my face. So intimate, everyone will see.
You are ready with your axe. What tricks we will perform together!
I will lie down. I'll lie quite still with my arms loose, waiting
for a miracle. For something extraordinary to occur.
When a hippo dies, the whole crash gathers in the water, watched
by white oxpeckers. The herd nudges the dead brown flanks
like a wedding silverside. Softly, they barge the corpse upriver
into the reeds. Then they begin licking. They lick the rough skin,
the hairs, the ear tips, its wounds. Nobody on earth can explain why.

Jessica Mookherjee

Skylarker on the 69 to Walthamstow

Full of Micky Bliss and Tom Tit, Betty gets back
with Vasilis and he shacks back in N seven, kicking off
to kopse the cornflakes on Lorraine Road, she moans
it's all Greek to her and he won't commit

though the sex is good, so asks me to live with her
near the reservoirs. Skint, even though they tell us
things can only get better, we're Brit-popped
and cidered in the Good Mixer, and *time-to-fly Angel*.

The truth is rent-rising and I, skylark turned magpie,
want all her hair-clips and shiny things. Marie says
don't go back green girl, keep step with the times.
So I go to the Dogs, to the roundabout rough land

ready for the big sky and the swing of air, they
say things are better now. We're at the East End,
E fifteen, need the 69 from Walthamstow to get home.
It rains and the market's full of plastic

and we look at each other and complain. I'm all
better now, I say to Marie and she gives me some plants,
a magic carpet and a gangster landlord counting cash
in the kitchen. I go to the forest where people disappear.

Manuela Moser

Notes towards France / a list of things that make me nervous

I wake up an hour later than intended

I think I am sitting next to a French man

I can feel him judging my croissant

It is quite clearly from Starbucks and tastes like cardboard

I feel myself beginning to judge my croissant

There are three women in the row behind me all wearing navy

but perhaps it's royal blue. Now I am second guessing myself

The woman in the middle sees me looking

I only looked round to see out of the window

It is raining

The rain streams across the window: we are moving

The woman on the left makes the sign of the cross, a child copies

The French man turns to me and says something French

It's more like an exclamation, but I can't speak French so let's just
say that he says something French and shrugs his shoulders

He looks excited as if it's his first time flying

If this is his first time then how did he get here?

I don't respond

I only suppose that he is French until now because he is wearing a stripy t-shirt and he has said something that sounded like French to me

The pilot is French

I spend the whole flight with headphones in trying not to listen to the French man talking to his companion just in case

The plane lands 24 minutes later than promised

I decide to ask the French people if they know the way to the train station

They are in fact French

They do not know the way to the train station

I tell them that I recently learnt to count to ten in French

They do not look impressed

I can see why: I can count to twenty in German

They seem about as fond of me as I am of my goldfish

The French man is laughing at me and I am only half sure why

It is a beautiful day and I want to make him laugh

I am glad that he is French and that he is wearing stripes

I am more disappointed than I would like to admit that his companion is not wearing stripes

I try not to let it show on my face

They say my future is to sit at the river's edge and look at the terraced houses

I suppose what they mean is that I am not going to catch my train

I am texting you and I miss my luggage

—run! she says

Outside the train window it all looks so French

Those farmhouses

Fields of sunflowers dying

Twenty aluminium poly-tunnel frames empty in the field

A spray of water in the middle of another field

A flock of sparrows that moves towards the spray

On thinking that those three things were so beautiful but only in their belongingness to each other in that moment

In the loneliness of singularity

In how obvious this thought is but how transcendent it felt at the time of thinking it

The silver, clear, blackness of it all

Daljit Nagra

Letter to Professor Walcott

Hardly worth *calling them out*, the old masters.
Each time a cause gains ground, should their estate
become glass house to alleged misdemeanours?
Their body of rhyme can be felt, it propagates
its own lineage. Should we read poems from a cave,
half-witted by the missing forefather? I stand before
the compressed volumes of verse across my shelves:
who covered their tracks, who'll outlive their flaws?

Who'd topple the marble of some national bard,
or gulag their name and the chela guarding them?
How many writers, the world over, are behind bars
for crossing a border of taste? It seems natural to harm
art and the artist. Consider Larkin whose private views
were amiss, who, if akin to his father's brown shirt,
who, if published by Old Possum who laid rats on Jews …
and I've lost myself, and the Work is no longer the work.

If influence imparts bad genes, who to weigh in the scales
of my nurture? Weigh Chaucer who forced a minor
into raptus? Weigh Milton mastering tongues to bate
his women like a whip? Weigh Coleridge pairing the horror
of Othello's wedded stares to those of a black mastiff?
Weigh Whitman and Tennyson who'd cleanse by skin?
If Kipling says we're devils, may I weigh the man of "If"?
How do I edit the Frost-like swamp I've swilled –

so many poets to recycle either side of this fireplace
before sweetness and light. Before I'm woke, in tune
with the differentiated rainbow and its crying flames.
Should I calmly cease their leasehold if they've abused
the canonical fortress? Or ride a kangaroo court
on its flood of Likes? Take down each Renaissance Man

to his manhood? But I hear the poems breathe: We can't
be judged by our birth, or judge our birth as Parnassian.

And you, dear Derek. Your Adam-songs for an island
sparked paradise from sanderling, breadfruit. Your spade
dug the manor and bones fell up. The senate columns
fanfared your arrival. They donned a black male
and colour was virtue. You opened my mouth and verse
came out. Your advocates cleaned your mess, their arms
held down the age, as though gods roamed the earth
to graduate girls. As though rape were the father of art.

You were "Dutch, n_____", Brit, you were my Everyman!
Why take on Caliban's revenge? Your moustache
a broom wedging its stanza of nightmare – in how many
Helens? Did you lust after lines inspired by whiplash,
taunted by sirens for your Homeric song? Intellectual
finger-jabbing seems off the mark: in the papers
Korean Ko Un's erased, and who'd fly to a terminal
if it was named for a serial pervert, Pablo Neruda?

I bet they hunt the dark man, Derek, in pantheon death.
Haunted or wreathed – how should you be honoured at
Inniskilling? Well, it seems fitting you fall in the West
where you carried "our" burden. Beside the foul spot,
I'd test my love again. You are in me: I'd never lose
you, if I tried. I'd begin with these, your old books, anew.
Now where on my shelves are you, travelling through
the old world? Where's your dog-eared *Don Juan*?

Doireann Ní Ghríofa

Escape: A Chorus in Capes

we are leaving our babies
fed and warm in their cots

we are leaving dark kitchens
untying apron knots

we are stumbling in nightdresses
through doors left unlocked

we are grasping towards water
past badger and fox

no moon, no, no star
when we wrench off our socks

only darkness so sharp
it fills pockets with rocks

we walk into rivers   we walk into seas
we walk into lakes   we will never speak

we are swallowed by water
we never will rise

we return through dark borders
leaving old lives behind

Jude Nutter

Disco Jesus and the Wavering Virgins in Berlin, 2011

> *Although a man, I no longer want.*
> *I disown and forget all desires of the flesh.*
> Late-Night Televangelist

How convenient, I say, to the dark. Because this
is what I do when I cannot sleep: sit in darkness
flicking through the god channels, sneering
and answering back, while the neon

tetras beneath their flickering tube light weave
their Möbius strip through the wet fire
of the only world they know; while a man
who makes it dishonest for a woman

to disown her desires—a man
whose body becomes, during sex,
one long wound—sleeps across the hall
in a king-size bed. Every scar is a door

and I have never known scars like his: shrapnel,
bullet, knife blade. The English, I told him
once, as I placed the welter of my lips to his damages
one by one, assume the French verb *blesser*—

to wound—means *to bless*; and he,
without remembering he said it,
said: *the way in and the way out—the doors*
to heaven are always small. This is a man who beguiles

even the dirt up from its knees, whose hands
conjure a body for me out of the body I have; and yet
every bed is a death bed; and yet, the only door
out of the body is death. Outside, a great city

and its troubled history under rain.
How is it we can be loved
so well and remain so famished still?
I rejoice, says the preacher, *in the celibate life*;

*the thought of one day dying
into heaven*. Behind him, deep in an alcove,
washed by slow strobes of alternating colour,
Jesus, life-size and on the cross, turns

from blue to red to yellow
and I am back, suddenly,
at those dreadful Youth Club discos—
all cheap lighting and tinny reverb

and hidden pints of liquor—where I
once let a boy called Martin nudge his hand,
centimetre by centimetre—as if
I would not notice—up under my blouse

until it came to rest, fingers spread, clamped
over my left breast like a fleshy starfish.
I let him because he was tall, a bad boy,
every girl's crush. And because my desire

was beginning to acquire a formal structure.
In this life, proclaims the preacher, as Jesus
turns yellow turns orange turns green, *we are all
under siege, beset by temptations*. I watch

as a single tetra, little morsel of colour, breaks
from the neon spackle of the crowd
and drifts upwards to place the dark foyer
of its tiny mouth

against the roof of its world. And what use,
really, is this life, if it's not one long
sheath of longing. *We are all under siege,*
he says, *afflicted, bedevilled, assailed*

by carnality, so let us pray. Let us pray, he says,
for the wavering virgins. Now I say
it is the poet's duty to wait,
to wait in the dark, to wait in the dark

at the world's mercy
for moments such as this. In the beginning
is the word. And the word
is sex. In the beginning is the kiss

that gives rise to the myth of Eden—that bright
landscape unfettered by history
that we create when placing our open mouth
to the open mouth of another

for the very first time. And yet there is
no garden in which the lion ever will
lie down with the lamb. And like this
the whole body becomes an eye turned

to nothing
but its own pleasure. And every time
we lie down to assuage our loneliness,
we find the flesh already there,

waiting. And all we ever want to do
is undo the violence of this world, and yet
that's how we lie down—with need
and avarice. In the beginning, as I remember it,

is a walled garden, staples of croquet hoops
punched into a lawn. Beyond, in a field,

a horse with a tail so long it brushes the grass.
Late summer. Farm work. Room and board

and pocket change for college. Summer's end,
then; cut fields at dusk and hawks slicing low
over the brittle blonde pipes of stubble.
So many lives already undone

by the round scythes of the combine.
At night from my single bed I listen to the pauses
and the breaks in the bicker of the shower
as the farmer's eldest son turns

and twists beneath it in the small bathroom
along the hall. When I imagine his body—which I do,
and often—it's as a series of broad,
quiet rooms inside the rattle of falling water.

He becomes a man made up of absence.
In the beginning (as I remember it) he puts on
his boots and waxed jacket and walks out
with his dog and a shotgun

into the fields. I do not remember
the gun's report, but if I am not with him
why are there pigeons, all flash
and clatter, breaking for the open; why do I feel,

still, the sudden change
in their purchase on the air—a few seconds
of wild churn and scramble before the spin down
into the stubble. There is the unlit weight

of each skull's chamber, the beak's
loose tweezers, the eyes' eclipse.
With the harvest in, with summer over,
with his parents at church again every Sunday,

it is inevitable, really. And afterwards we lie
like moist kindling under the covers and the world
is just as it was, only more so.
Over the fields, first mists of September

unfurling their aprons the colour of iron.
Rooks like black static. A breeze heckling
silver out of the grass until the lawn
is a carpet of knives. It is my job to cut and split

and ransack the nave of each bird,
which his mother will bake with orange juice
and honey. Six birds in a wheel
on a willow pattern plate, a carousel

of pigeons, their bald, glazed wings
like tiny flippers, and what meat there is
latticed by shot. It is 1978. I am eighteen.
The year Sweden outlaws aerosols,

and Markov, Bulgarian defector, is assassinated
with a poisoned umbrella tip, and Egypt
makes peace with Israel and war begins
in Afghanistan and a man more than twice my age

teaches me that the body
is its own reward. And these days
I sleep right through the minor disruption
of my lover's shower, and when I wake

he's at work—in jeans, perhaps, but shaved—
with his feet on the table and a folder
of case notes before him and his gun, unbreakable
heart, in a holster against his ribs. *The hungers*

of the body, says the preacher, *always*
lead us astray. So let us pray.

Outside, the red crumble of tail lights
down Linienstraße. A great city

and its troubled history under rain.
The whole of Europe under the same rain.
A *waver*, I once read, is a young tree
left uncut during the clearing of timber. Rain,

somewhere, loosening its clothes to play wanton
in the fields; rain drumming its fingers
on the green tiers of the trees. The loneliness
of rain that has come so far

touching only one leaf. And where rain is falling
where there are no leaves, a greater loneliness.
Every word for what we are
leads us back to this. *Human*,

from the Latin *humus*, meaning earth. *Flesh*,
from the Greek, related to *sarx*, meaning earthly; meaning,
of man set adrift from the divine. Every word
for what we are brings us back to the dirt. *So yes*, I say,

let us pray. Let there be buttons
abandoning their buttonholes. Let tongues unbuckle,
let watches, let belts. May small change fallen
from pockets be forgotten, never found.

And shy flags of hair swing loose. Storms
inside strokes of wind. The world is full
of alchemy, so let there be questions
and demands. Small talk, dirty talk, language

in all denominations. Let keys drop and fingers find
every latch and lock and legs peel free
from the sheer, long throats of stockings. Let hearts
be up to their necks in longing.

May jackets and shirts turn inside out;
may the body—in rooms specially rented,
in cars, on tables, in single beds
on Sundays. *Body*, believed to be related to Old Norse

buthker, meaning box; as in, coffin
that goes into the earth. And when the virgins
go down may they go down like heavy crops
go down before the cutter—without choice

and ripe with rains and sugar. Jesus, abandoned
on the cross, alone in his alcove, turns
from green, back to blue, back to red,
while in its tank that single tetra forms perfect

circles on the water simply by drifting
to the surface and kissing what imprisons it.
Why, if desire is so perilous, are we given a god
so obviously human, with an athlete's body, lean

and well-worked; a god whose loincloth is slipping,
pulled down by its own slight weight
over one hip; who has, still, despite all
that's been done to him, such beautiful hands.

A god whose crown is askew,
whose hair needs washing, whose wounds
will become the most terrible of scars.
A god who may well

have desired a woman who made desire pay.
Who may well have been her lover.
Who dies with his arms wide open.

Abigail Parry

In the dream of the cold restaurant

the man with the buttonhole and broad lapels
is folding and refolding a white napkin.
Look, say his hands, at intervals. A swan.
A dancing girl. An intricate scale model
of the Maughan Library on Chancery Lane.
The man adjusts his buttonhole and coughs

as each one fails, precisely, to entertain.
A waitress intervenes, bringing two plates –
fluted, plain, translucent. And quite empty.
Such is the gaunt extravagance of dreams.
That waitress, though. All elbows, wrists
and hips. A strip of exposed skin reveals a scar

on the nub of bone that finishes the spine.
No – not a scar. A burn. A full-blown wet rosette,
just like the one you earned at seventeen
from a fuck on a nylon carpet – a carpet
not unlike this carpet here, lalling its beige
hoops and braids around the table's feet.

Meanwhile, on the mezzanine,
someone lifts a book and reads the line
he left his knee exposed, and dreamed
of travelling on a mail coach by night.
Well quite. When you offer up your plate
it turns, beneath your hands, to a crumpled swan.

The man, of course, has gone.
Such is the glib economy of dreams.
So find a way to bear it, if you can –
the man who folds and folds and cannot please,
the cheap carpet, telling its idiot riddle,
the girl who has not learned to move between

compassion and contempt. But then,
other people's dreams are very dull,
as the waitress knows with all the brutal
certainty of being seventeen. And she's gone too.
She'll pull this city to the ground before
she'll take your plate, let alone your pity.

Eleanor Penny

Winter, a biography

I'll admit I was raised in a red house by a woman with red hands
on a bare hill, where birds walked on the ground and it was
always winter and death did not exist. She never married. She
knelt down on the ice. Her mouth red as an axe swung through
the stomach of a cat. She held a handful of seeds. She buried
them and expected nothing. Death did not exist. I couldn't read
but I nailed the book through its heart to a tree, and waited.
Spring's surrender flag rippled alabaster in the distance. Sharp
sigh of horizon. Winter a thin murmur of bone. You were there
too, admit it. The brittle child of us riding the same song witless
and burning to the old bridge like a stolen car. Stars, waterlogged
and filthy in the river. Glossy, bloated nettles humming by the
road. Every Saturday a man in a red coat measured the shape of
our skulls. Every tree had a someone to climb it with a dishcloth
in their mouth to wipe its shining branches leafless, black. I held
the weight of snow in my arms like a sleeping animal. We drove
unwatched across the border.

Full knuckled summer struck me speechless. Forgive me if I've
been a stranger here. Once again it's winter, and you can sleep
in my arms like snow.

Rowan Ricardo Phillips

November Nocturne

I looked out over the cool rising night,
Its soft froth of lamplight and scrubbed-out stars
Tumbling out over the blue tub, mind's sky,
Cash-only bars, evening everlasting,
Triumphant Brooklyn barely visible
Tucked behind the East River like the hem
Let out of an iridescent dress culled
To continue being the verse, the harm,
The wine-tonned mouth swollen with the last words
Of Spring or April or Night or The Plain
Sense of Things, the worlds in it burning, ways
Of I am now burning, feeling the Bern
In the back of a cab without being burned,
Then being burned. I wonder what I learned.

Richard Price

Personality Test
with worked examples

Are you made of
dogs
fogs
or cogs?

Son: dogs.
Father: fogs.

Are you made of
cats
splats
or rats?

Son: splats.
Father: cats/rats.

Are you made of
sticks
tricks
or licks?

Father: tricks.
Son: licks.

Are you
lights
tights
or fights?

Father: lights.
Son: fights.

Son: you're tights.
Father: lights.
Son: he's tights.

Are you
        bones
        phones
        or moans?

Father: phones.
Son: moans.

Are you
        playing
        saying
        or neighing?

Son: saying.
Father: neighing.

Are you made of
                coasts
                boasts
                or ghosts?

Son: coasts.
Father: ghosts.

Are you made of
                board games
                band names
                or old flames?

Father: band names / old flames
Son: board games

Are you
        a note pad
        an iPad
        or a launch pad?

Father: a launch pad.
Son: iPad.
Son: he's a note pad.

Are you
        country walks
        serious talks
        magic bean stalks?

Son: serious talks.
Father: You are not serious talks! You are magic bean stalks.
Son: serious talks.
[   ]
Father: I'm country walks.

Do you practise
                stagecraft
                witchcraft
                or Minecraft?

Father: witchcraft.
Son: Minecraft.

Are you
        asks
        tasks
        or masks?

Son: asks.
Father: tasks/masks.

Are you
       sneezes
       teases
       or pleases

Father: teases / pleases.
Son: sneezes.

Are you afraid of
          locks
          rocks
          or socks?

Son: locks.
Father: locks.

Father: you're also afraid of socks.
Son: just locks.

Yousif M Qasmiyeh

If this is my face, so be it

Walking alongside his shadow, he suddenly realised that it was both of them who needed to cross the border.

They fortified their walls with cement and nails. They moved their women and children to a safe place and shouted: They are coming after our faces; they are coming after our crops!

Immemorial is the smell of refugees.

The equivalence of a refugee would be his body.

Wake! He said to his body when they arrived. A bit of air was in the air.

The child has become water... It is to the side, a tad clear, a tad not, but when you look him in the eye you will see the meaning of water.

Whoever can sense the coming is a refugee. The refugee can neither come nor depart; he is the God of gestures.

We might also say: The face is a dead God.

Whoever claims asylum, whoever lends his hands to his strangers so they could bear out his presence and his things, is the one who has many deities and none.

Refugees and gods always compete for the same space.

What is intimate is the face and never the refugee.

The refugee is only intimate in his death and if there is only one death to ponder, it is that of the refugee.

If this is my face, so be it. For once, it is a stone's throw away.

A being with cracked soles is Man.

The refugee is the superimposed being. Not only does he act as an alibi to existence, he also creates existence. Without the refugee, existence is no longer existent.

Refugees, to kill time, count their dead.

Killing time is the correlative to killing themselves.

A no-place is what substantiates a deceased refugee.

A death with no place can never happen.

A refugee only returns to bear witness to his own return.

In the absence of time, arrival takes place.

Claiming asylum always results in the overreading of the proper noun.

This happens when it is enough to say that it is the body that claims asylum. The body by itself. The body as its body. Whatever state it is in, it is the body, the body in the flesh, that submits itself in front of other bodies, in order, first and foremost, to be declared present, made present, or to be seen as such by those with more mature flesh and finer cuts. In the flesh, the refugee arrives while bearing witness to his own body, while holding the narrative of the body: I am sacrificing my body for myself; nobody and nothing else, to edge back into the ladder of bodies and be a sign amidst signs. The body is by itself; bare, melancholic as the body in its first outing. Whatever state it is in, it is that that carries all states to the threshold. To the borderline whose remnant is a body and whose body is a remnant. In the flesh is what the refugee can see with or without the gaze.

Only those who have never seen a place can describe the place.

Those who flee their homes tend to have faces that are slightly clearer than the moon. In the above clarity, only the face can substitute its creator.

In asylum, we borrow our bodies for the last time.

Whenever my mother wanted to leave the house, it was to see God's face. God's face, according to her, was somewhere else.

Man, how is it that your body is intact?

The refugee is he who fears himself. When the self is deafeningly mauled, he will fear the place but never the animal.

There is nothing sacred about the sacred save the eyes.

On the threshold, they slaughtered us and time.

Yvonne Reddick

Storm Petrel

He departed to raise the Jurassic.
The hill-wind on my father's face, before weeks
aboard the rig. North of the peak
where the road would end, spent Sunday
trudging to the Nevis cairn.

The pilot made him walk a line.
'Drysuit? Lifejacket?'
– 'Check.'
'Reddick?'
– 'Ready!'
The rotor-blades split air.
He watched cities shrinking:
Stonehaven, Peterhead,
Aberdeenshire's rain-grey granites.

Over the waves, the blade of Shetland.
They named the metal oil-platforms
for birds: Merlin, Osprey, Brent.
He stepped onto the platform, for
the two-week static voyage.

Storm petrel, Cape Verde coast

So seabound, she stumbled on land –
tough light approaching, though
days were no longer.
Dust hazing the air, dust
in the petrel's throat and feathers;
sand clouding the sea where she dived.
By the rock-caves, fishermen with their catch
of conches sat on hot stones,
cracking the chambers of shells.

The Sahara had flown to
sea on the Harmattan –
the conch-fishers scarved
their eyes to watch the petrels
patter wings and feet on waves,
stepping north on water.

Dunlin A platform

The rig-lights fiery on choppy breakers.
In his bunk, sardine-canned
with four dorm-mates,
my father lay restive under a thin blanket.

Noise jackhammered everyone's eardrums –
drilled through cabins,
girders. Dad felt the weather turn.
The men perched

over an ocean above
a deeper ocean of sweet, black oil.
The rig boomed like a petrol tanker,
its hull pitching over the North Atlantic.

Dinner was mock chop, double chips and peas,
then double chips and peas with mock chop again.
Failure to hold the handrail
was a sackable offence.
My father learnt how
to say *No sé hablar Español*
at night classes. Workers on
an iron-and-concrete outcrop
need instructive hobbies. They miss
their women, their families, grow fractious –

Storm petrel, North Atlantic

Scavenging flotsam:
shrimps, krill, moon jellyfish,
those translucent creatures
called *by-the-wind sailors*.

Petrels can smell oil a mile off,
will scrounge whale blubber
or scraps from a salmon farm.

They follow in the wake of trawlers.

Dunlin A platform

A favourite pastime is birding. Blown off course,
birds are enticed by rig-lights. They know
these angular sea-rocks
gather rainwater. 'One morning,'
my father said, 'an osprey,
right up there on the crown block.'

Other émigrés: fieldfares, bramblings,
the injured short-eared owl that flew
landward in the helicopter with the drilling crew.

A seal that surfaced and offered a sardine
to the scaffolder on the abseil line –
they locked gazes, eyes round as portholes.

The best was the corncrake
rasping by the draw-works –
all hundred and two men
raised their glasses of Kaliber.

Storm petrel, North Atlantic

The petrel was heading for Mousa,
that crumb of rock holding

her nest in the prehistoric cairn.
She and her mate would tend
a quartz-white egg,
each parent brooding the warm, live pebble,
before the weather turned and they
returned to the Cape Verde winter.

Dunlin A platform

Wind woke and filled its lungs.
Three-metre waves slammed the legs
of Dunlin A. The flame blown backwards
down the steel throat of the flarestack dragon.
Whiplash rain, near-horizontal.
A crackle on the intercom:
Deck's slippery, boys!

No-one slept that night: the storm bawled
through chinks in cabins, and rain
battered its fists on the roof. The rig
an ocean liner, tethered but foundering.

Bloodshot sky that morning; the blown gale sullen.
The men went on deck to hand-line for mackerel.
My father told me, with a catch
in his throat, of the disgorger,
the gaff, their dulling eyes.
A gift of slick-blue bodies for my mother
when he returned, the red
wound in each hulled belly.

Storm petrel, Dunlin A platform

At the first whiff of fish-guts
they arrived like a squall:
the flock treading water
to the rig with its sea-legs.

One of them crash-landed by the galley.
Draggled feathers; only her head moved,
flicking right and left in panic.
The rig cook, once a ship's chef,
offered leftover cod.
'It's a petrel. Never seen them so early.
Sailors say they bring heavy weather.'

My father cradled the exhausted traveller,
lighter than the balsa glider he assembled
as a boy. He ran his fingers
along the wire-like struts of wing-bones,
checked the ruddering tail, the submarine keel-bone
and launched the storm-petrel
into unsettled sky.

Christopher Reid

Death of a Barber

Not Mustafa, but one of his colleagues
cut my hair today.
That's when I learned that Mustafa
had passed away,
a victim of the virus.

Intimate work, the barber's:
fingers, scissors and razor
titivating
with professional gentleness
crown, sides, back and neck.
Almost a caress.

I had been going for ages
to the little shop he used to have,
festooned with climbing plants
and budgerigars in cages,
before I learned Mustafa's name
and something of his life;
but, as etymology tells us,
touch and tact are the same.

For months now, no one had touched me
except my wife,
and I was looking forward
to a needed trim.
I got one, as expert and luxurious
as any of Mustafa's,
but it was not from him.

Matthew Rice

Aniseed

In the school canteen
I watched you
take your knife

and crack that last sweet
down the middle,
marvelling at the seed

embedded in its candy core,
our tongues rusted red.
In the strong sunlight

that scrutinised the sachets
of mayonnaise
and ketchup,

I'd been thinking of
that morning's history lesson,
the martyrdom of Thomas Becket,

the blood white with the brain,
the brain no less red from the blood,
my mouth cathedraled

with the memory of aniseed,
the angles of cutlery,
the sun's stealth attack

across your blank expression.

Michael Symmons Roberts

Beheading the Horse

Once the last of the sawing is done,
bone uncoupled from bone
neck's latch lifted from its shoulders
as if to leave a centaur

half-built on the cold-stone flags,
I light up, take a drag,
turn my back on the cobalt eye
that gawps up from the floor at me.

I wrap the head in my old trenchcoat,
lay it on the passenger seat,
then strike out down unlit back roads,
to the motorway. It's good,

I tell myself, to find such a perfect head
for the job. That being said,
it makes a disconcerting fellow traveller
and this odyssey will take me hours.

Fog-lights on. My nerves are shot.
The radio keeps cutting out
so nothing in my car can drown
this awkward, shifty one-to-one.

I swear I keep seeing it flinch
every time I clear my throat,
or retch. I'm gagging on its stench
as it bleeds on my beige bucket-seat.

Then the coat slips off: one naked
eye stares up from the sheer
Vantablack chasm of this head,
as if someone cut a tan leather

horse-face mask, leaving me this horror.
I'm lost in the middle of nowhere,
when, no lie, this beast begins to talk.
I'd like to say its homily was hindmilk,

that it led me into some repentance.
In truth it was just nonsense.

Robin Robertson

By Clachan Bridge

I remember the girl
with the hare-lip
down by Clachan Bridge,
cutting up fish
to see how they worked;
by morning's end her nails
were black red, her hands
all sequined silver.
She unpuzzled rabbits
to a rickle of bones;
dipped into a dormouse
for the pip of its heart.
She'd open everything,
that girl.
They say they found
wax dolls in her wall,
poppets full of human hair,
but I'd say they're wrong.
What's true is
that the blacksmith's son,
the simpleton,
came down here once
and fathomed her.
Claimed she licked him
clean as a whistle.
I remember the tiny stars
of her hands around her belly
as it grew and grew, and how
after a year, nothing came.
How she said it was still there,
inside her, a stone-baby.
And how I saw her wrists
bangled with scars

and those hands flittering
at her throat,
to the plectrum of bone
she'd hung there.
As to what happened
to the blacksmith's boy,
no one knows
and I'll keep my tongue.
Last thing I heard, the starlings
had started
to mimic her crying,
and she'd found how to fly.

Declan Ryan

Mayfly

On the way back to the city after the long weekend, we stop off
by prior agreement at The Mayfly, arrange ourselves like
collapsed parachutists.
Last of the nectar days, hide-end of the country, the afternoon
readying itself to make excuses and leave us to our unslept
dishevelment.
Some nameless river goes by; the sun makes brilliant hoops from
tarnished glasses. Half-picked bones; soporific bluebottles.
To have to leave this
for the road's demands, the mercy of one last round not enough
to delay us where people live their whole lives, most likely,
watch this cherry tree convulse into winter, what, seventy times
maybe.

Maria Stadnicka

Homología

Father, who art in Heaven,
I bought a derelict church
and converted the building into
a battery farm. Every eight weeks

a hatchery truck delivers me
blackbirds to feed – grow – slaughter.
I'm led into temptation, spend nights
smothered in feather-filled dreams.

I trespass, forget the heating in the barn
and beaks clutter the ventilation valves.
Deliver me now from Evil. Father, I spotted
a black mark and cut my earlobe off;

now my child's cry sounds mono
in a faraway room. Someone has built
a wall of flesh between us. *You can hear
much clearer once the pain dies down.*

Sister knows which lie sounds better
at regular check-ups – *Eat your fruit* –
but I find baby teeth buried
in each apple. One bite, and seeds fall

on my breast, swell like a season.
My skin breaks out in black patches,
shoots sprout from my arms, seep out
the milk holding my bones together

with my flesh. Buds and twigs push
my ribs further apart. A child-tree grows
in my chest, claims its sliver of meat,
humming litanies to an adult-fruit.

Father, they signed me up for research
and as soon as the paperwork passed
the Ethics Committee they asked for
samples of tissue from my left eye.

Sacrifice my vision in the name of science,
check my womb for blackness but say *Black*
only if you really mean it. Father, we all eat
pasta with mud and no-one complains that

the earth lacks seasoning. Yes, please, I need
another portion of this, sleep-walk
into the garden, repeat instructions
from qualified staff: *Take a deep breath!*
                    Take a deep breath!
                                Amen.

Joelle Taylor

Valentine

Born right body
wrong day, Valentine
flicks her lighter
in the corner of the club
& white women flutter.
Tonight, she has dressed
as the inside of a mouth
a handsewn suit excised
from a cured night sky
black leather has its own skin
care routine it listens
to its mother I have heard
it said some girls give birth
to themselves on the back
of motorbikes invent the wind
let the road uncurl from between
their legs, the infinite motorway
something British & unbidden
i know why we are drawn
to the corners it's where the road
cannot reach us. Every part
of a woman is a weapon
if you know how to hold it
Valentine says. The corner
flicks a Morse & in the dark
white hearts beat like moths
against a headlight.

GC Waldrep

Broken Things
Morwenstow

You stow them to the rear of worship: bits of jagged iron,
candle-nubs, miscellaneous gears and levers, each perfect
unto itself but useless apart from its fellows. The human
back is meant to bear this weight: cable spools, dusty
vases. Here is a picture of Christ, and here is a picture of
Christ. Imagine the eyes first, oblique timepieces upon
which vision prints. I cough up a tooth, mature and perfect.
It glistens in my hand. The chancel remains locked,
nursing its treasures with a dim milk. I can just feel the
tooth resting in the center of my palm; I shift it slightly,
its planes mazing the half-light. Is it broken, I ask myself.
Is it worship. Every century or four someone scrubs the
images from the walls and replaces them with new images.
A fish. A crown. A scythe. See, this special niche for
books from which pages have been torn. You may open
and close them: an almanac, a lab manual, a toddler's
pop-up fable. In my hand I am still holding this single
tooth, which my body offered up. It is not, to my knowledge,
mine. I imagine the dark chancel full of teeth, a mouth
sewn shut. GO FIND OUT THE ARROWS instructs
the legend in the glass, that falls on me. Nowhere is there
speech or talk of mending. A child's collage, a cracked
slate. I can't decide where to leave the tooth: in the Lady
Chapel, by the font, at the ad hoc altar to war veterans
in the north aisle. The tooth requires neither assembly nor
instruction. It is a cool kernel in my outstretched hand.
So I swallow the tooth. In this way I turn my back on
worship. I take it with me, away from the splintered table-
leg, the xylophone missing a key, the saints' tongues,
the floral wire, old kneelers with their stuffing leaking out.
Easter baskets, water pitchers. The damaged umbrellas.

Rushika Wick

519 People

519 people died whilst at their work desks this year. The statistics reveal that employees who had been at the same workplace for more than ten years were ten times more likely to expire in this manner, and that more artists in their 'day jobs' died than any other category of primary occupation. A team of scientists analysed the position of the bodies as found on the desks:

60% were reaching out for something in the moment, 21% writing reports that appeared to be turning into poems and 10% had been trying to leave their desks. 9% had disappeared within the minute after death. In these cases, there was a very faint outline of the body in fine ochre dust, and the scent of violets. The first person to pass away in this manner was writing a treatise on "Making a Fool of Death" complete with woodblock illustrations from an unpublished 18th Century Hungarian occult manual. In this arresting work, small men with elongated noses enter into discourse with winged mice. In a double-page spread entitled Underworld of Labour, there sits below the floor of a wedding banquet hundreds of bent figures toiling over production of armour and weaponry, their gaunt rib-cages and perpetually hungry eyes gleaming in the pale light. At the bottom right of this picture, women try to – pass themselves off as men, betrayed by escaping breasts and grabbed at by other workers.

The last person to die in this manner within the financial year was a fine artist working as a paralegal in The City. The night before she died, she was working in oils on a self-portrait, wearing an exquisite floral coronet of cosmos and floating grass-heads (which remains unfinished).

The advice for concerned readers is to consider hot-desking and drink green tea, high in antioxidants.

A relaxation app linked to this study is also available to purchase.

Biographies of the shortlisted writers

Forward Prize for Best Collection

Kayo Chingonyi (b. 1987, Mufulira, Zambia) moved to the UK aged six after the death of his father. When he was 13, he lost his mother, around whose absence many of the poems in *A Blood Condition* (and his debut, *Kumukanda*) revolve. Chingonyi's work is meditative and lyrical: 'It's gratifying to know that the kind of work which is my wheelhouse, which is sometimes considered quiet, subtle, understated, can still resonate,' he writes in response to his shortlisting.

Chingonyi lives in West Yorkshire and teaches Creative Writing at Durham University. Newcastle was his first destination after leaving the Copperbelt of Zambia, and many of the poems in *A Blood Condition* focus Chingonyi's deft eye for place on the northeast of England: 'the part of me / lost to the realm / of ledgers / of legend' ('a northerly aspect').

Tishani Doshi (b. 1975, Chennai, India) found her poetic feet while training as a dancer. 'I learned about breath, stamina, flexion, time, rhythm, control, discipline,' she writes, 'and I also received the subject that would be the centerpiece of all my explorations: the body.' She has pursued this subject through four full collections, beginning in 2006 with the appropriately titled *Countries of the Body*, winner of the Forward Prize for Best First Collection.

A God at the Door continues this focus on embodiment; poems take on the shapes of their subjects – a fir tree, a pair of speedos, an ambiguous 'bird or flower' – while, in poems like 'Why the Brazilian Butt Lift Won't Save Us', Doshi interrogates beauty norms with caustic, irreverent humour. She lives in a coastal village in Tamil Nadu, where the name of her beachside house, Ar Lan y Môr ('Beside the Sea'), provides a physical expression of her Welsh-Gujarati heritage.

Selima Hill (b. 1945, London, UK) builds up her collections from characteristic sequences of short, disturbing lyrics, each a brief glance then a turning-away from a central subject: in the case of *Men Who Feed Pigeons*, seven different men and their relationships with women.

(A companion book with the sexes reversed, *Dressed and Sobbing*, is forthcoming from Bloodaxe in 2023.) What redeems her work from bleakness is Hill's knack for manipulating surreal imagery, and her sense of humour, which is unlike anything else in contemporary British poetry.

Hill was born into a family of artists: 'I am only a writer in as much as I am not a painter or musician like the rest of my family,' she writes. 'I thought writing was more cool because it was less public.' Her advice for poets starting out today is pragmatic: 'Sweep the floor; clear the workspace; don't have one more coffee.'

Luke Kennard (b. 1981, Kingston-upon-Thames, UK) writes poems which are by turns tender and hilarious, playing with voice and tone; he can be disarmingly self-deprecating but, as Caroline Bird writes, he 'has the uncanny genius of being able to stick a knife in your heart with such originality and verve that you start thinking "aren't knives fascinating… and hearts, my god!" whilst everything slowly goes black'.

Notes on the Sonnets is a collection of responses to Shakespeare's sonnets, which form (in Kennard's words) 'a strange, dreamlike narrative set at the same house party' where he began writing the sequence. He is currently working on another long sequence, *Jonah*, a follow-up to 2016's *Cain*, which Alan Hollinghurst described as 'the cleverest and funniest thing I've read all year'.

Stephen Sexton (b. 1988, Belfast, Northern Ireland, UK) won the Forward Prize for Best First Collection in 2019 for *If All the World and Love Were Young*, which he describes as 'more a project book or concept album' than *Cheryl's Destinies*. 'Generally speaking,' he writes, *Cheryl's Destinies* is a collection of poems 'trying to articulate, in some way or another, how the imagination responds to stress, how it comforts and preserves itself.'

This idea of preservation is a central part of Sexton's poetic practice; *Cheryl's Destinies* ends with a long elegy for his early mentor Ciaran Carson, an accumulation of quotidian details and minutiae, trying to hold on to 'those afternoons of etymology / in small back rooms both dishabille and elegant'. Sexton's poems are firmly rooted in the geography and physicality of Belfast, where he was born and still lives.

Felix Dennis Prize for Best First Collection

Caleb Femi (b. 1990, Kano, Nigeria) was London's first Young People's Laureate. He is a film-maker and photographer as well as a poet, and his own photos – of the places and faces of the North Peckham estate, where Femi's imagination finds its jumping-off point – are scattered throughout the pages of *Poor*.

Femi's poetry both bears witness and celebrates resilience in the face of urban poverty; he describes it as 'an endeavour to articulate the lives and times of my community of North Peckham'. This community included the murdered schoolboy Damilola Taylor, whom Femi knew and to whom one of the central poems in the collection, 'How to Pronounce: Peckham', is dedicated. In an interview with the *Guardian*, Femi describes the contrasts of life on the estate: 'The conditions of the estate – poor public housing, poor design – did have the knock-on effect of being quite dark. But the young people within it are joyous and full of imagination. They embrace fantasy.'

Alice Hiller (b. 1964, Singapore) began writing poetry aged 50, following treatment for ovarian cancer. 'Being cut open to remove the tumour somehow gave me permission to open up the subject of childhood abuse – which shame and silence had held within me,' Hiller writes. 'I wanted to give creative witness to the crime to which I had been subjected.' The result was her debut collection, *bird of winter*.

Hiller is adept at dealing with difficult material: she founded a workshop collective called 'Voicing the Silence' and runs an interview series called 'saying the difficult thing' to encourage other poets writing through similar traumas. Her strategies include transforming found materials from Pompeii and Herculaneum – excavations which become a natural metaphor for her own excavation of her past – and hand-made erasures, 'each made over the course of a single intense day, with multiple redrawings'.

Cynthia Miller (b. 1992, Kuching, Malaysia) wrote most of the poems in *Honorifics* during the 'heady first-lockdown blur' of summer 2020, having taken a poetry course which provided rapid-fire daily prompts. 'I tend to have fallow years where I don't write anything at all, so I've had to train myself to write rapidly when it does come,' she writes. 'Like a horse that's already running away and I'm just hanging onto a fistful of mane for dear life.'

Miller's subject-matter includes motherhood, migration and her mixed Chinese-Malaysian heritage, as well as an electrifying sequence on jellyfish. Like the metaphysical poets of the 17th century, she draws her metaphors from everywhere: popular science, cookbooks, sci-fi films. Describing what she most values in the work of her favourite poets, she mentions a restlessness, an alertness, a sense that you never quite 'know whether you're going to be sucker punched, seduced or startled by the next line'.

Holly Pester (b. 1982, Colchester, UK) began writing poetry when she was a receptionist in her early twenties 'and would do anything to make the time go by'. She went on from there to the East London experimental art and poetry scene, making DIY books for zine bookshops, and reading and performing with props including an electric hand-whisk and a homemade harp. 'I've done a lot of things and publications already, sound works, performances, chapbooks, radio works, talks, events, works that have completely disappeared now,' Pester writes. 'It's lovely to work in an unprofessional order!'

In a 2019 essay, 'The Politics of Delivery (Against Poet Voice)', Pester describes a radical prosody, one which 'creates spaces and moments for what can be said. The poets I listen out for recreate that space through an insubordinate rhythm against the condition of the day.' *Comic Timing* enacts that description, creating a space for rage, for the 'bodily-yet-politicised experience'.

Ralf Webb (b. 1991, Bath, UK) was managing editor of *The White Review* from 2017 to 2021. *Rotten Days in Late Summer* is constructed around three sequences: 'Diagnostics', about a father's death from cancer and its aftermath; 'Treetops', exploring Webb's own struggles with mental health, and the 'Love Stories', which are scattered throughout the collection and deal with the yearning and pathos of different relationships.

Webb stresses the communitarian aspects of poetry: 'Even if the act of putting pen to paper (or fingers to keyboard) might be done alone, there is so much more that can be done with others to contextualise or inform that act,' he writes. His own work in this area includes the Arts Council-funded *PoetryxClass* reading group project, which he set up and ran, focusing on the intersection between poetry and class identities.

Forward Prize for Best Single Poem

Fiona Benson (b. 1978, Wroughton, UK) won the Forward Prize for Best Collection in 2019 with *Vertigo & Ghost*, a collection whose central sequence was an astonishingly vivid reworking of Greek myth. Her forthcoming collection from Cape, *Ephemeron*, also features a long mythic sequence from which her shortlisted poem 'Androgeus' is drawn. 'It is a retelling of the minotaur myth, which tries to reinstate Pasiphaë, the minotaur's mother, at the centre of the story,' writes Benson. 'Androgeus is her firstborn son, who is killed by a bull in mainland Greece.'

'Androgeus' and the sequence to which it belongs were written during the first lockdown in 2020. 'I thought at the time that I was indulging in a great act of escapism, travelling in my imagination to sundrenched Greece. But looking back at them, they are all about being trapped.'

Natalie Linh Bolderston (b. 1995, Stoke-on-Trent, UK) published her first pamphlet, *The Protection of Ghosts*, in 2019. She is currently working on her debut collection, heavily informed by family history: her mother and grandmother were Vietnamese-Chinese refugees who fled to the UK.

'I chose to write about this using my middle name because it's part of my identity – the only part of my name that acknowledges my Vietnamese heritage,' she writes. 'Writing about diacritics was also a political choice. In a climate where English is often treated as the superior language and many people are made to suffer for using their native languages, I wanted to resist these racist attitudes by centring and celebrating the beauty and uniqueness of Vietnamese.'

John McCullough (b. 1978, Watford, UK) wrote 'Flower of Sulphur' immediately after taking a year off from poetry owing to ill health after the publication of his third collection, *Reckless Paper Birds*. 'When I returned, I felt suddenly able to tackle areas I'd found too painful to write about before, using experimental forms,' he writes.

McCullough's PhD at the University of Sussex was on friendship in English Renaissance writing; 'Flower of Sulphur' returns to his experience of study, a breakdown and a friend's suicide. It is self-referential, commenting on its own forms – commonplace book, abecedary, game – while remaining heartbreakingly direct. 'Poetry for me is a craft and like any craft it takes thousands of hours of quiet honing. There's no way around this,' McCullough writes. 'I guess my biggest piece of advice to anyone starting out in poetry is try to enjoy the journey of discovering writers who reshape the way you see the world and each little breakthrough as you refine your editing strategies.'

Denise Riley (b. 1948, Carlisle, UK) is a philosopher and feminist theorist as well as an admired poet. She's written eight works of non-fiction, including the influential *'Am I That Name?': Feminism and the Category of 'Women' in History*, and in 2012 won the Forward Prize for Best Single Poem with 'A Part Song'. Her *Selected Poems* were published in 2019 by Picador.

'The title of my poem "1948" marks a particular patch of British post-war social history: the treatment of "illegitimate" children by the various authorities concerned,' writes Riley. '1948 was the year of my birth; this poem's also a directly personal account – which I feel jumpy about. But despite my strong misgivings, I've tried to brace myself against the exposure of publishing it, because in the current climate of social amnesia, it may shed some light on half-forgotten institutional systems of "care" policies and their repercussions, and so it could resonate with the many older people who were similarly and silently affected.'

Nicole Sealey (b. 1979, St Thomas, US Virgin Islands) began making erasures from the United States Department of Justice's 2015 report detailing bias policing and court practices in the city of Ferguson, Missouri, three years after the murder of Michael Brown by Ferguson police: her shortlisted poem is an excerpt from this much longer work.

Sealey's erasures leave the original report's stilted, bureaucratic language still readable in grey; the flashes of lyric which appear inside it become a commentary on the suffering and lived experience the report suppresses. 'Being shortlisted for the Forward Prizes is a huge honor,' writes Sealey. 'This means a larger audience for this work. A larger audience for this work may mean more eyes on The Ferguson Report. More eyes on the Report may mean more honest conversations about bias policing. This is the hope.'

Publisher acknowledgements

Jason Allen-Paisant · On Property · *Thinking with Trees* · Carcanet

Threa Almontaser · And That Fast, You're Thinking about Their Bodies · *The Wild Fox of Yemen* · Picador Poetry

Tiffany Atkinson · Clean windows · *Lumen* · Bloodaxe Books

Khairani Barokka · in which i hypnotise a tiger · *Ultimatum Orangutan* · Nine Arches Press

Alex Bell · Arkteia · *PERVERSE*

Fiona Benson · Androgeus · *Times Literary Supplement*

Leo Boix · Meditations of an Immigrant (Cinquaines) · *Ballad of a Happy Immigrant* · Chatto & Windus

Natalie Linh Bolderston · Middle Name with Diacritics · National Poetry Competition

Elizabeth-Jane Burnett · Barrel Jellyfish · *Of Sea* · Penned in the Margins

Dom Bury · The Opened Field · *Rite of Passage* · Bloodaxe Books

Lewis Buxton · Taxidermy · *Boy in Various Poses* · Nine Arches Press

Anne Carson · Sure, I Was Loved · *Times Literary Supplement*

Sumita Chakraborty · O Spirit: Of Moby Dick · *Arrow* · Carcanet

John Challis · The Last Good Market · *The Resurrectionists* · Bloodaxe Books

Kayo Chingonyi · The last night of my 20s · Origin Myth – Miguel · *A Blood Condition* · Chatto & Windus

Suzanne Cleary · For the Poet Who Writes to Me While Standing in Line at CVS, Waiting for His Mother's Prescription · The Moth Poetry Prize, *The Moth*

David Constantine · Jimmy Knight · *The North Magazine* · The Poetry Business

Polina Cosgrave · My People · *My Name Is* · Dedalus Press

Tishani Doshi · After a Shooting in a Maternity Clinic in Kabul · Mandala · *A God at the Door* · Bloodaxe Books

Maia Elsner · After Auden's 'Musée des Beaux Arts' · *overrun by wild boars* · flipped eye publishing

Martina Evans · Hackney Trident · *American Mules* · Carcanet

Kit Fan · Suddenly · *Poetry Ireland Review*

Joseph Fasano · Letter to Lorca Written on His Piano, Granada, 2019 · *The Scores*

Caleb Femi · Boys in Hoodies · Things I Have Stolen · *Poor* ·
Penguin Books

Annie Freud · Rimbaud's Ovaries – A Mondegreen for Our Times ·
Hiddensee · Picador Poetry

Angela Gardner · Shoddy Tarnished Gifts · *The Sorry Tale of the
Mignonette* · Shearsman Books

Alan Gillis · The Readiness · *The Readiness* · Picador Poetry

Jen Hadfield · Dolmen · *The Stone Age* · Picador Poetry

Maryam Hessavi · Red Cities · *PN Review*

Selima Hill · The Beautiful Man Whose Name I Can't Pronounce ·
Wedding Cake · *Men Who Feed Pigeons* · Bloodaxe Books

Alice Hiller · o dog of pompeii · valentine · *bird of winter* · Pavilion Poetry

Luke Kennard · 'How heavy do I journey on the way' (50) · 'Then let not
winter's ragged hand deface' (6) · *Notes on the Sonnets* ·
Penned in the Margins

Victoria Kennefick · Beached Whale · *Eat or We Both Starve* · Carcanet

Fran Lock · La jena di Londra · *Poetry London*

lisa luxx · for a subculture to resist capitalist co-opting it must remain
impossible to define · *fetch your mother's heart* · Out-Spoken Press

Gail McConnell · 'The Clouded Border I like best' · *The Sun is Open* ·
Penned in the Margins

John McCullough · Flower of Sulphur · *Poetry London*

Andrew McMillan · pill-box · *pandemonium* · Jonathan Cape

Alexandra Melville · Hippo · *The Moth*

Cynthia Miller · Sonnet with lighthouses · To become a dragon first wear
its skin · *Honorifics* · Nine Arches Press

Jessica Mookherjee · Skylarker on the 69 to Walthamstow ·
Finished Creatures

Manuela Moser · Notes towards France / a list of things that make me
nervous · *The Stinging Fly*

Daljit Nagra · Letter to Professor Walcott · *Times Literary Supplement*

Doireann Ní Ghríofa · Escape: A Chorus in Capes · *To Star in the Dark* ·
Dedalus Press

Jude Nutter · Disco Jesus and the Wavering Virgins, Berlin, 2011 · *Dead
Reckoning* · Salmon Poetry

Abigail Parry · In the dream of the cold restaurant · The Moth Poetry
Prize, *The Moth*

Eleanor Penny · Winter, a biography · Poetry London Prize 2020,
   Poetry London
Holly Pester · Blood · *Villette* · *Comic Timing* · Granta Poetry
Rowan Ricardo Phillips · November Nocturne · *Living Weapon* ·
   Faber & Faber
Richard Price · Personality Test · *And Other Poems*
Yousif M Qasmiyeh · If this is my face, so be it · *Writing the Camp* ·
   Broken Sleep Books
Yvonne Reddick · Storm Petrel · *Ambit Magazine*
Christopher Reid · Death of a Barber · *The Late Sun* · Faber & Faber
Matthew Rice · Aniseed · *The Last Weather Observer* ·
   Summer Palace Press
Denise Riley · 1948 · *Poetry Ireland Review*
Michael Symmons Roberts · Beheading the Horse · *Ransom* ·
   Jonathan Cape
Robin Robertson · By Clachan Bridge · *Grimoire* · Picador Poetry
Declan Ryan · Mayfly · *Times Literary Supplement*
Nicole Sealey · Pages 22-29, *an excerpt from* The Ferguson Report: An
   Erasure · *Poetry London*
Stephen Sexton · The Curfew · High School Musical · *Cheryl's Destinies* ·
   Penguin Books
Maria Stadnicka · Homología · *Buried Gods Metal Prophets* ·
   Guillemot Press
Joelle Taylor · Valentine · *C+NTO: and other poems* · Saqi Books t/a
   The Westbourne Press
GC Waldrep · Broken Things · *The Earliest Witnesses* · Carcanet
Ralf Webb · Aktiengesellschaft, Wiltshire · Love Story: Crown of Love ·
   Rotten Days in Late Summer · Penguin Books
Rushika Wick · 519 People · *Afterlife as Trash* · Verve Poetry Press

Winners of the Forward Prizes

Best Collection

2020 · Caroline Bird · *The Air Year* · Carcanet

2019 · Fiona Benson · *Vertigo & Ghost* · Cape Poetry

2018 · Danez Smith · *Don't Call Us Dead* · Chatto & Windus

2017 · Sinéad Morrissey · *On Balance* · Carcanet

2016 · Vahni Capildeo · *Measures of Expatriation* · Carcanet

2015 · Claudia Rankine · *Citizen: An American Lyric* · Penguin Books

2014 · Kei Miller · *The Cartographer Tries to Map a Way to Zion* · Carcanet

2013 · Michael Symmons Roberts · *Drysalter* · Cape Poetry

2012 · Jorie Graham · *PLACE* · Carcanet

2011 · John Burnside · *Black Cat Bone* · Cape Poetry

2010 · Seamus Heaney · *Human Chain* · Faber & Faber

2009 · Don Paterson · *Rain* · Faber & Faber

2008 · Mick Imlah · *The Lost Leader* · Faber & Faber

2007 · Sean O'Brien · *The Drowned Book* · Picador Poetry

2006 · Robin Robertson · *Swithering* · Picador Poetry

2005 · David Harsent · *Legion* · Faber & Faber

2004 · Kathleen Jamie · *The Tree House* · Picador Poetry

2003 · Ciaran Carson · *Breaking News* · The Gallery Press

2002 · Peter Porter · *Max is Missing* · Picador Poetry

2001 · Sean O'Brien · *Downriver* · Picador Poetry

2000 · Michael Donaghy · *Conjure* · Picador Poetry

1999 · Jo Shapcott · *My Life Asleep* · OUP

1998 · Ted Hughes · *Birthday Letters* · Faber & Faber

1997 · Jamie McKendrick · *The Marble Fly* · OUP

1996 · John Fuller · *Stones and Fires* · Chatto & Windus

1995 · Sean O'Brien · *Ghost Train* · OUP

1994 · Alan Jenkins · *Harm* · Chatto & Windus

1993 · Carol Ann Duffy · *Mean Time* · Anvil Press

1992 · Thom Gunn · *The Man with Night Sweats* · Faber & Faber

Best First Collection

2020 · Will Harris · *Rendang* · Granta

2019 · Stephen Sexton · *If All the World and Love Were Young* · Penguin Books

2018 · Phoebe Power · *Shrines of Upper Austria* · Carcanet
2017 · Ocean Vuong · *Night Sky with Exit Wounds* · Cape Poetry
2016 · Tiphanie Yanique · *Wife* · Peepal Tree
2015 · Mona Arshi · *Small Hands* · Pavilion Poetry
2014 · Liz Berry · *Black Country* · Chatto & Windus
2013 · Emily Berry · *Dear Boy* · Faber & Faber
2012 · Sam Riviere · *81 Austerities* · Faber & Faber
2011 · Rachael Boast · *Sidereal* · Picador Poetry
2010 · Hilary Menos · *Berg* · Seren
2009 · Emma Jones · *The Striped World* · Faber & Faber
2008 · Kathryn Simmonds · *Sunday at the Skin Launderette* · Seren
2007 · Daljit Nagra · *Look We Have Coming to Dover!* · Faber & Faber
2006 · Tishani Doshi · *Countries of the Body* · Aark Arts
2005 · Helen Farish · *Intimates* · Cape Poetry
2004 · Leontia Flynn · *These Days* · Cape Poetry
2003 · AB Jackson · *Fire Stations* · Anvil Press
2002 · Tom French · *Touching the Bones* · The Gallery Press
2001 · John Stammers · *Panoramic Lounge-Bar* · Picador Poetry
2000 · Andrew Waterhouse · *In* · The Rialto
1999 · Nick Drake · *The Man in the White Suit* · Bloodaxe Books
1998 · Paul Farley · *The Boy from the Chemist is Here to See You* ·
Picador Poetry
1997 · Robin Robertson · *A Painted Field* · Picador Poetry
1996 · Kate Clanchy · *Slattern* · Chatto & Windus
1995 · Jane Duran · *Breathe Now, Breathe* · Enitharmon
1994 · Kwame Dawes · *Progeny of Air* · Peepal Tree
1993 · Don Paterson · *Nil Nil* · Faber & Faber
1992 · Simon Armitage · *Kid* · Faber & Faber

Best Single Poem
2020 · Malika Booker · The Little Miracles · *Magma Poetry*
2019 · Parwana Fayyaz · Forty Names · *PN Review*
2018 · Liz Berry · The Republic of Motherhood · *Granta*
2017 · Ian Patterson · The Plenty of Nothing · *PN Review*
2016 · Sasha Dugdale · Joy · *PN Review*
2015 · Claire Harman · The Mighty Hudson · *Times Literary Supplement*
2014 · Stephen Santus · In a Restaurant · Bridport Prize

Supporting Poetry with Forward

Proceeds from the sale of this book benefit the charity Forward Arts Foundation. Forward believes everyone should have the opportunity to develop creativity and agency by making, experiencing and sharing poetry.

We aim to promote public knowledge, understanding and enjoyment of poetry in the UK and Ireland. We are committed to widening poetry's audience, honouring achievement and supporting talent. Our programmes include National Poetry Day, the Forward Prizes for Poetry and the Forward Book of Poetry, an annual anthology of the year's best poems.

Our mission is:
- To celebrate excellence in poetry
- To increase poetry's audience
- To deepen appreciation of poetry's role

To find out more, visit our website forwardartsfoundation.org and follow us on Facebook or Twitter @ForwardPrizes.